JESUS
- OUR -
MESSIAH

JESUS
- OUR -
MESSIAH

From the Covenant to the Cross

RICHARD N. FYFFE

TATE PUBLISHING
AND ENTERPRISES, LLC

Published by Tate Publishing & Enterprises, LLC
127 E. Trade Center Terrace | Mustang, Oklahoma 73064 USA
1.888.361.9473 | www.tatepublishing.com

Tate Publishing is committed to excellence in the publishing industry. The company reflects the philosophy established by the founders, based on Psalm 68:11,
"The Lord gave the word and great was the company of those who published it."

Book design copyright © 2016 by Tate Publishing, LLC. All rights reserved.
Cover design by Samson Lim
Interior design by Gram Telen

Published in the United States of America

ISBN: 978-1-68333-513-9
1. Religion / Christian Theology / General
2. Religion / Christian Education / General
16.05.19

Acknowledgements

This book would never have been written without the encouragement, support, and expertise of my wife Danielle. She believed in me and envisioned my becoming an author years before I did. She has served as collaborator, editor, and literary consultant throughout the process. She was patient when I wasn't. She was an IT and software specialist when I was clueless. And she was tireless in her assistance when I ran into barriers time and again. Thanks Babe.

Deep appreciation goes out to the leaders of the church I serve. My Holy Land travels, made possible by their generosity and support, have deeply enhanced my faith and richly blessed my ministry. Finally, I want to thank my church, the Southeast Church of Christ. Their enthusiastic support for a series of lessons I presented, "Our Spiritual Roots," gave me a reason to write. Thanks folks.

—Rick Fyffe

Contents

Part I

The Need for the Messiah

1

In the Beginning, Messiah

Learning the Basics

Early one Saturday in the summer of 1964, my brothers and I were rudely awakened by these loudly spoken words, "Get up, boys. It's time to work." Reluctantly, we got up, got dressed, and were ushered out the front door without so much as a bowl of cereal. My dad was doing the loud talking, hurried ushering, and being way too enthusiastic about it. None of this was in any way interesting because we knew. He had been prepping us all week for "big-project Saturday." There was lots of yard work, the pool needed cleaning, and a whole long list of other chores. But mostly, we were dreading the mess waiting for us in the garage. It seemed odd that he led us out the front door since the back patio was the quickest route. But it didn't make any difference; we certainly weren't in any hurry. We stood there sleepily, resenting the rude awakening and loathing the long and miserable day ahead of us.

We barely muffled our groans as Dad lifted the garage door, for we knew what awaited us. There were mounds of clutter, tools on the floor, and piles of unfinished projects. All the chaos was our doing. The devastation that three boys can create in one garage boggles the mind. Especially egregious to my dad was the mess we left for someone else to clean up, namely him. Guess what? On that sleepy Saturday morning, we were someone else.

But as our eyes adjusted to the dim light, they began bulging out of our heads. We weren't seeing an avalanche of clutter. Instead, there before us was a sight we would never forget—three bright and shiny bicycles. These were bikes in the new style of tall handlebars, long "banana" seats, and sissy bars! These were cool bikes, the bikes the cool kids owned. Taped across the handlebars was a banner, "Happy Birthday, Boys."

My older brothers, having revived from their shock, mounted up and pedaled off. But me, well, I didn't know how to mount up, for that gorgeous piece of machinery was my first bike. Dad spared me the indignity of training wheels, which was great, but that meant I would have to learn to ride. I was small for my age, and with the seat at its lowest, I still couldn't pedal all the way around. So Dad attached blocks to the pedals, and I was ready to go! It was not to be a day of deadly projects. There would be no yard work, pool cleaning, or the long list of chores. Instead of being dreadful, it turned out to be one of the greatest days of my life.

My parents and I walked the bike to the vacant lot across the street, an excellent place for lessons. It was epic. We quickly developed a working rhythm: Dad got me going with a push, let go, and I would fall over. This repeated a number of times and wasn't the best part of my day. But I figured it out. After mastering balance, I learned how to keep moving, to keep pedaling after he let go. Once I had forward momentum, I moved on to braking, which was great because I kept crashing onto the neighbor's fence. Then there was steering as I, several times, drifted into the street. My mom's shrieking was helpful. But eventually it all came together: balance, pedaling, braking, and steering, which resulted in not falling, crashing, or drifting into the street.

By lunch, I was caked in dust and felt ready to get out on the street with my brothers. But it would be a few days, and that vacant lot and I became good friends. That was all right because I was a kid with a cool bike and was on my way to some glorious times. In the following weeks, I learned to pop wheelies, jump ramps, and do some tricks. The best part was riding around the neighborhood with my friends, which we did for hours and hours through the hot summer months.

Thinking back, there were some key elements to my success that day. I had a committed and patient teacher who taught me solid fundamentals. Learning the basics of balance, pedaling, steering, and braking were essential for successful bike riding. And that was way more fun than falling, crashing, and Mom shrieking. I learned that focused, forward motion was the best way to get where I was going. It turned out those lessons had value for other areas of my life.

The Spiritual Life

Like many believers, I was raised in church; some might say I was yanked up. A friend of mine says he was attending church for months before he was even born. In our faith fellowship, most of the teaching and preaching came from the book of Acts, the Letters of Paul, and then from Peter and John, and maybe James. Largely ignored were the Gospels, Revelation, and basically the Old Testament. Most of the lessons addressed the topics of salvation and worship and stemmed from the texts regarding these important doctrines. For us, the New Testament—and not all of the New Testament—was used to prove our primary points of faith and practice.

Over time, it seemed to me that the Old Testament was more than just missing; it had become something akin to a worn-out lawn mower. In my family, when the lawn mower wore out, we bought a new one. The old one was kept out back behind the garage. We thought of it as a second hand, backup mower. Actually, the old one was seldom, if ever, used. Why use a worn-out mower when a new and better one was sitting in the garage?

So why was the Old Testament (OT) ignored? Well, because we thought of it as old, worn out, and not of much use. I was taught that "the OT was nailed to the cross, and was no longer relevant, no longer needed." It's curious that somehow the Old Covenant became synonymous with the Old Testament. As if the books of law were all there was to the OT. In practice, it seemed that the "old book" was gone and forgotten. The exception was, of course, the books of poetry.

I'll never forget the chiding I received as a young preacher for occasionally preaching from the OT. Each time I did, one of my good members would come up after the service, get in my face, and say, "Brother Fyffe, we don't need any preaching from the old book. It was nailed to the cross, and we just don't need it anymore. Stop preaching from the Old Testament." You may find it highly improbable that someone would say that to me, but they did, and not just once. In time, I gave in and gave up teaching from the OT.

And if that wasn't bad enough, as mentioned above, my Bible education contained very little of the four Gospels. I knew the stories but emerged having never grasped how the stories fit together or what value the stories held in relation to all of scripture. I didn't know that each Gospel emphasized a different perspective of the Messiah. In my family, we were strictly Acts and Epistle Christians. We were New Covenant, New Testament believers.

A deeper understanding would come later, much later. The journey required an exploration into ideas and concepts beyond what I had learned. The path led me to Israel and the Holy Land several times. It would involve years of fresh and challenging study, a study of the entire Bible.

The journey led me to the OT and unveiled the Messiah and his ministry. Messianic prophecy wasn't new to me, but whatever I had learned was precious little compared to what could be learned. A strong investment into the law, the psalms, and the prophets was deeply challenging, and the awareness of how much I had missed was a stunning discovery.

Basically, I realized that everything Jesus did and taught was rooted in the OT. This awareness created a new conviction: If I am to know and accurately apply the teachings of Acts and the Epistles, I must first have a deeper understanding of Jesus and his teaching. And a deeper grasp of his teaching can only come from a comprehensive knowledge of the law, the psalms, and the prophets.

A weak knowledge of the OT will likely result in a skewed understanding and produce some erroneous conclusions of Jesus's teaching. Like a half-finished painting, the reader may emerge with only a partial view. It did for me. It's like trying to understand a book with sixty-six chapters by starting in the fortieth chapter. Along the way, you discover many hard-to-understand texts, some confusing passages, and even whole books that make no sense. Typically, we just filled in the blanks with thoughts or ideas that seemed to fit, not smart. Trying to understand the Word with whole sections of missed knowledge is like trying to ride a bike without handlebars and a missing pedal. You can probably ride the bike, but not well, effectively, or safely.

My understanding of the OT was weak, especially the prophets. I had not studied them with the same passion as I had the NT letters. You see, I was an Acts and Epistle Christian and an Acts and Epistle preacher.

We need to understand that Jesus, our Messiah, fulfilled everything that his Father planned from the beginning. This understanding allows us to see the deeper connection between the Old and the New, to see how they align so beautifully and join together seamlessly. I hope to infuse you with a deeper appreciation for Jesus of Nazareth and to help you connect even more to the heart of Jesus.

Much like learning to ride a bike, we need to start at the starting place, to learn our fundamentals. By seeing how God worked in the writings of the Old Testament, we can move forward to Jesus, our Messiah, the Savior of our souls.

Before moving on, here a few thoughts about Old Testament prophecy.

Understanding the prophets can be frustrating. Some of the frustration comes from thinking that there will be a single, easily identified point derived from a straightforward interpretation. Sometimes our interpretations are built on the idea that prophecy should make sense immediately at the first reading. Some of us may approach prophecy with the expectation of it being clear, logical, and will fit in with my beliefs. Do I have the right to such expectations?[1] Is that the best approach?

As a modern, Western Gentile, I have a habit of trying to box my beliefs. What is that, you ask? Well, it's my way of interpreting a text, deciding on its primary meaning, then reducing it down to a simple conclusion. "I get it, I have it, this fits my understanding and makes sense," I say to myself. Upon capturing its meaning, I put it in a box and place it on a shelf. It's boxing theology or "theology in a box." It's a common approach to Bible study, but not always effective, especially with the OT prophets. It really doesn't work well with the prophet Zechariah.

The prophets were written with "layers" of meaning, and their writings can have multiple interpretations. If this makes reading the prophets difficult, well, the problem isn't with the text; it's with the reader. I'm not suggesting that the prophets are beyond comprehension. Prophetic scriptures were immersed in Jewish history, the Hebrew culture, and in a writing style reflective of the ancient authors.

The prophets wrote in poetic style. Their text was often written in picture form, with deep symbolism, and their writings could communicate in and out of the past, present, and future. To gain a better grasp of the prophets is to gain a better understanding of Hebrew thought.[2] The better I understand the Hebraic element of the text, the better my understanding of the text. To truly grasp the prophets, I have to get into the mind of the prophet, to see how he wrote and why he wrote it. I need more time with the Hebrew text, not less.

The writings of Torah and the Psalms and the prophets are profitable and beautiful and so amazingly beneficial for faith and a richer relationship with God. To see Jesus, our Messiah, in his fullness and glory is to see him first revealed in the Hebrew text. There must be a deeper knowledge of the Old Testament before we can effectively understand the Jesus of the New Testament. As believers, we need to grow in our ability to read, study, and understand the amazing writings of the prophets.

2

Abram's Unintended Covenant

Have you ever given your word and then had to break it? Breaking a vow or a promise can be very disappointing to others, and sometimes devastating. I find that I'm bothered more when others break their promises to me than when I do it to them. That's not right, is it? Keeping our promises should be a sacred responsibility, especially when they are made to family.

One day, my five-year-old daughter came up to me and, in her sweetest voice, asked if she could have a dog. With my kindest voice, I told her no. She asked me every day, and every day I said no. This went on for a while until she finally said, "Dad, why can't I have a dog?" I counted off the reasons: puppies are hard to train, you have to clean up after them, we don't have a fenced backyard or a doghouse, and mostly they can be really expensive. Her reply was, "How much would I need to buy a dog?" I threw out a number that was sure to dash her puppy hopes for good. "Fifty dollars," I said. "So if I save fifty dollars, I can have a dog?" she asked. "Yep, absolutely, if you save fifty dollars, I will get you a dog." She looked up at me, smiled, and walked away.

Time rolled by, and I forgot about the dog. Then one day, about eleven months later, she came running up to me and said, "Dad, I have the fifty dollars. You promised I could have a dog, so you'll keep your promise, right?" I couldn't believe the dog topic had surfaced again. So I asked to see the money. She opened a small bag containing a bunch of ones and fives and a lot of change. I counted it, and yep, she had it. I was struggling to accept how this child had saved up fifty dollars on her meager allowance and money earned from extra chores. But she did. By eight o'clock that night, we had a dog, a rescue puppy, a golden retriever she named Mitzi.

I considered any number of ways to break my word, to do it gently and gracefully, but to definitely get out of the promise. But I couldn't; I had given her my word. Actually, it was more like a covenant. If she provided the money, then I would provide the dog. Those were the terms, the exchange made by oath. Yes, it was only a pet, but for my daughter, her dad's integrity and the value of his word hung in the balance. Promises, agreements, and covenants—they are made with heartfelt trust and exist to be fulfilled.

From the Hebrew Text

Abram and the Promises of God

Abram's story began in the city of Ur in ancient Mesopotamia, in the part of the world we know as southern Iraq. Ur was a city infused with idol worship. For one example, they were moon worshipers, and we would think of them as pagan. Terah, Abram's father, most likely raised his family in idolatry and may have been an idol maker. What is unclear or unknown is when God first revealed himself to Abram, but at some point in Abram's life, God established a connection with him, and he began to follow God.

At the close of Genesis 11, Terah made the decision to take his family and possessions and go to Canaan. They headed north, following the route with the freshwater rivers, until they reached Haran. They settled there for some time, and during their stay in Haran, Terah died and was buried.

God's Call to Abram

In Genesis 12:1–3, God called to Abram in Haran to take his wife, family, and possessions and go to Canaan. He was seventy-five years old when he left. But before he did, the Lord made three profound and amazing promises to him:

1. That his descendants would become a great nation
2. That his descendants would inherit the land of Canaan
3. That one of his descendants would bless the nations of the world

As Abram journeyed south to Canaan, he carried those promises with him. But the promises remained a mystery. After settling in Canaan, the years passed. Abram was getting older and remained without children, without a male heir. It seemed unlikely that the descendants God had promised him would ever be a great nation, and so how could they ever inherit Canaan as a lasting possession. Abram was growing tired of waiting on the Lord, and in his discouragement, he began doubting God. When the Lord repeated the promises to Abram, he responded by asking for signs that would serve as proof. Abram would receive two signs that served to confirm the promises. They were given to reassure Abram and restore his confidence. The signs would be powerful, and one of them extremely graphic. But Abram asked, and God responded. Abram received his signs, but I'm not sure he was ready for the second one.

The First Sign: Stars in the Sky

> But Abram said, "O Sovereign Lord, what can you give me since I remain childless and the one who will inherit my estate is Eliezer of Damascus?" And Abram said, "You have given me no children; so a servant in my household will be my heir." (Genesis 12:2–3)

In response, God took Abram outside to give him a glorious illustration regarding the future of his people. He had him look up at the innumerable stars in the night sky and assured Abram that his offspring would be as numerous as the stars[1] (Genesis 12:4–5). The text recorded that Abram believed God and that his belief was credited to him as righteousness. This was groundbreaking, truly amazing stuff, and not just for Abram but for the entire world. God demonstrated His willingness to impart righteousness to those who believe, who have faith.[2]

The Second Sign: The Blood Covenant

Abram chose to believe God regarding his descendants; apparently, the stars served to convince him. But as for the land promise, Abram felt the need to press a little harder.

> He also said to him, "I am the Lord, who brought you out of Ur of the Chaldeans to give you this land to take possession of it." But Abram said, "O Sovereign Lord, how can I know that I will gain possession of it?" (Genesis 12:7–8)

A fairly bold question, don't you think? For who was Abram to question God?

So in response to Abram's request for a second sign, the Lord initiated with him a common and revered ceremony known as the blood covenant or the blood path.

> So the Lord said to him, "Bring me a heifer, a goat and a ram, each three years old, along with a dove and a young pigeon." (Genesis 15:9)

This was quite a response to Abram's question, "O Sovereign Lord, how can I know that I will gain possession of it?" I paraphrase, "Here is what I want you to do, Abram. Go get these five animals and bring them back to me." Without further instructions, Abram brought the animals, slaughtered them, and then arranged them in a very specific way, none of which God told him to do, at least not in the text. I believe Abram was well acquainted with the ceremony of the blood path, and when God instructed him to bring the animals, he knew exactly what to do and what was about to happen. But I'm also offering the idea that the blood covenant (BC) wasn't what he had in mind when he said to God, "Lord, how can I know that I will gain possession of it?" The BC would bring Abram into a much more serious position with God. You might say it turned out to be Abram's unintended covenant.

Here is what happened next:

> Abram brought all these to him, cut them in two and arranged the halves opposite each other; the birds, however, he did not cut in half. Then birds of prey came down on the carcasses, but Abram drove them away. (Genesis 15:10–11)

Then Abram fell into a deep sleep and God spoke to him in a dream.

> As the sun was setting, Abram fell into a deep sleep, and a thick and dreadful darkness came over him. Then the Lord said to him, "Know for certain that for four hundred years your descendants will be strangers in a country not their own, and that they will be enslaved and mistreated there. But I will punish the nation they serve as slaves, and afterward they will come out with great possessions." (Genesis 15:12–14)

> When the sun had set and darkness had fallen, a smoking firepot with a blazing torch appeared and passed between the pieces. On that day the Lord made a covenant with Abram and said, "To your descendants I give this land." (Genesis 15:17–18)

What was that all about? What did it mean? What's the significance of the smoking firepot and blazing torch?

The BC was no ordinary agreement, no common promise. It was serious, significant, and much grander in scope. Abram probably didn't realize it at the time, but the covenant God was about to make with him would affect the salvation of the world. It would have direct implication for the third promise that a descendent of Abram's would bless the world.

Let's take a look at this strange and bloody ritual.

History of the Blood Covenant

The BC was an ancient practice. Between 2000–1500 BC, it was used among tribal leaders, heads of families, and village leaders. It was used to resolve disputes and settle issues related to land exchange, rights of way, water rights, military conflicts, and to establish peace between tribes, villages, and even between families. Does using blood to make peace remind you of anyone?

The Fundamentals of the Blood Covenant

The Hebrew word for *covenant* means "to cut" or "cut where the blood flows." The covenant's conditions were solemnized and sealed in blood, both human and animal. The cutting and subsequent death of the animals represented a serious and sacred moment between those forming the covenant. Life was ended so a relationship could begin.

The Blood Covenant's Ceremony

- The two parties would meet in an open field. If the covenant were between villages or tribes, then a representative from their bloodlines was sent.

- The ceremony began with verbal exchanges of the covenant's conditions, the promise and responsibilities for each party.

- The covenant was sealed in blood[3]. The parties stood opposite each other with the animals between them, the animals' throats slit and placed on their backs to be cut from the neck down through the belly. It's called a blood path for a reason. Imagine the blood pooled around the animals.

- The two parties then took turns walking through the blood on one side of the animals and then returned on the other side. Their feet, ankles, and lower legs would be covered or least splattered with blood. The two parties both shared equally in the death of the animals.

- Each party then took a knife and made a cut on their right wrist. They then clasped forearms so their blood flowed into each other. They were covenant partners by blood, bound to each other in a relationship that was considered stronger than family. Then they returned to their places.

- Still facing each other, they raised their right hands and swore an oath to keep the conditions. They might have said something like, "I will keep the conditions of this covenant until my death. If I break this covenant, you may do this to me." The words varied or changed due to culture and the passing of time. But the message was clear: "If I violate this oath, you may cut me open and walk in my blood."

- Then they shared a meal with witnesses. The food may have been as simple as bread and wine. In the ancient Eastern cultures, bread represented the flesh, and the wine represented the blood. The meal symbolized the relationship, the bond and unity between them.

- The final element was to make exchanges with each other. They might have exchanged an article of clothing like a cloak or robe, perhaps belts, and weapons that would hang or fit in a belt. They would give to each other a part of their name, so each one had a new name that included the identity of their covenant partner. Lastly, they might exchange their oldest male son who would then live and stay with the other's family.

Returning to God, Abram, and the Covenant

The whole experience was purposed in demonstrating God's will that Abram inheriting Canaan was absolute. It was a promise sealed in blood, a covenant partnership stronger than anything Abram would have imagined could happen.

The message Abram received in the vision, while sleeping, was of two powerful symbols of God's presence: the blazing torch and smoking firepot. Some examples include God revealing himself at Mount Sinai by fire and the mountain being covered in smoke. The pillar of cloud guided the Israelites by day and the pillar of fire by night. God demonstrated His presence in the tabernacle and temple by the burning incense and the cloud of smoke, the sweet-smelling sacrifice of praise.

The reason for two symbols was that God provided one for Abram and one for Himself. Abram would not be required to walk the blood path. The symbols passed over and around the animal carcasses, representing both God and Abram in the blood path.

In their covenant, God and Abram exchanged names. Abram received the *H*, the primary letter in *Yahweh*, or *YHWH*. *Abram* was changed to *Abraham*. God took Abram's name, as seen in the reference "the God of Abraham." They also exchanged their oldest sons: Isaac to be sacrificed on Mount Moriah and Jesus to be sacrificed at Calvary. Isaac being spared at the last moment was a picture of the BC. God provided a substitute so Isaac didn't have to die. He would provide a substitute so we didn't have to die. God's merciful substitution was revealed early on in scripture. The parallels between God and Abraham, between Isaac and Jesus, just go on and on.

God provided assurance to Abram that his descendants would increase in number through looking at the night sky. Through the BC, he demonstrated that they would absolutely inherit the Promise Land. But before they could, they would first be enslaved for four hundred years. Then God would bring them out. And eventually, under Joshua, they inherited Canaan, and the land promise was fulfilled.

But the spiritual promise would come later. It would find its fulfillment through Isaac, Jacob, the tribe of Judah and David, and ultimately with Jesus, the lion of the tribe of Judah, the son of David. The Messiah would come and would be the heir who blessed the nations. But again, that would come later. Before it did, God required something from Abraham.

God Requires Blamelessness

The blood covenant required nothing from Abram at that time. But God did include a covenant condition.

> When Abram was ninety-nine years old, the Lord appeared to him and said, "I am God Almighty; walk before me faithfully and be blameless. Then I will confirm my covenant between me and you and will greatly increase your numbers." (Genesis 17:1–2)

Abraham was required to walk before God and be blameless; this was the condition for confirming the covenant. The great and sobering effect was this: "Abraham, if you fail to walk before me blamelessly, or if your descendants fail, then I can cut your throat and stomp in your blood."[4] When Abram said to God, "How can I know?" I'm not sure that he was asking for something as serious, graphic, and strong as the blood covenant; for he if he did, then he and his descendants would have a very difficult requirement—to be blameless.

Of course, God knew that neither Abram nor his descendants would live blamelessly. I believe this is why He provided both symbols in the blood covenant ceremony. It was God's way of saying that when the time came for Abram and his descendants to be held accountable for not walking blamelessly, He would provide a substitute.

Someone else would stand for Abram's guilt and would shed blood for Abram's failure.[5] Someone else would die.

At just the right time, God gave his Son for the world. At Calvary, He demonstrated the amazing grace that was promised in Genesis 12: "And through your seed all nations of the earth will be blessed."

In fulfilling the blood path, God introduced a new covenant, a better one. Not another covenant of animals slaughtered and their blood pooling. No, this would be a better covenant, of the Spirit, and built on better promises.

From the Greek Text

Jesus and the Passover Week

Now let's roll forward about 1900 years to Jesus and the Holy City of Jerusalem. It was Passover week, his last Passover, and he was there with his disciples. Jesus spent his final days teaching in the temple courts, and at night, he went to the Mount of Olives and to Bethany, the village of Martha, Mary, and Lazarus. Each morning, he returned to Jerusalem and to its overwhelming number of worshipers present for Passover and the Feast of Unleavened Bread. The temple pulsed with activity; the city vibrated with anticipation. And Judaism's highest leaders were immersed in the plot to kill Jesus.

Each day, the morning and midafternoon sacrifices were offered. They were even more significant because of the great feast, the celebration of God passing over the houses of their ancestors and sparing their firstborn sons (Exodus 11:5). For each of the two daily sacrifices, a spotless lamb was selected, brought to the killing place, and prepared for slaughter. At the giving of the signal, a priest up on the temple wall blew the shofar, a signal to all that it was time for the sacrifice. The lamb's life was forfeit. It was a sacrifice for the sins of the people, as if they were each saying to God, "Thank you for sparing us, for not demanding justice for our not walking blamelessly before you, and thank you for not cutting our throats and walking in our blood."

Since the Law of Moses, lambs had been slaughtered, their blood shed and their bodies burned to God. Why were these animals sacrificed twice a day? The justice and righteousness of God demanded satisfaction. The lambs were offered so God would not hold the people accountable for breaking the covenant, for not living blamelessly before him. So it was twice a day, day after day, and year after year. But the time for God to fulfill the blood covenant was near; it was close at hand.

Jesus was arrested while praying in the garden of Gethsemane. He was put on trial, lasting through the night. The high priest declared him guilty and worthy of death, and he was sent to the Roman governor. Pilate found him innocent and wanted to release him, but the people demanded his death; they cried out for it. Pilate attempted to pacify the crowd by having Jesus scourged, but it wasn't enough. They wanted him dead; and quickly, for that day was a special Passover Sabbath. It would be essential for Jesus to die and be removed from the cross before sundown.

"Shall I crucify your king?" Pilate asked. "We have no king but Caesar," they replied. So off they went to execute the King of kings. At about three in the afternoon, about the time for the afternoon sacrifice, a priest went up on the wall, blew the shofar, and the lamb's throat was cut. Somewhere close, just outside the city wall, Jesus cried out, "It is finished." The Lamb of God was slain, and in that moment, the blood covenant made 1800 years earlier was fulfilled.

God was faithful to His promises: Abram received his heir, his descendants became a nation, and they inherited the Promise Land. But Abram failed to walk blamelessly before God, and so did his people, and so did I. But God would not hold Abram accountable. He would not walk in his blood. Instead, He provided the lamb whose blood was given for Abram's failures and our own.

The blood of the Lamb that took away the sin of the world wasn't a late-arriving idea, nor was it an unfortunate anomaly. The blood was foreseen and intentional. Nearly 2000 years before Jesus was sacrificed, his Father made a covenant with Abram and offered both parts of the oath so neither Abram nor his descendants would ever be held accountable for their sins. This was God's grace in the blood covenant, His sending his representative, His oldest male son, to cover our sins. God's representative would ultimately die in our place so we didn't have to.

James L. Garlow and Rob Price in *The Blood Covenant* say,

> Let us close this book by saying that we have never heard of the covenant being kept by any human; but on the part of God the Father and on the part of his Son Jesus Christ, we have never heard of the covenant being broken. At its heart, the covenant is an expression of God's faithful, enduring love, demonstrated unsurpassably in the death of Christ, from which flows reconciliation, relationship, authority, and may treasure more. The covenant was not merely made, it was lovingly kept for you and for us, and we enjoy the inexplicable benefits of it.[6]

For Us Today

For more than thirty years, I read Genesis but never paused to consider the strange verses of chapter 15. It's only been in the last few years that this beautiful text has opened up its amazing picture of amazing grace. Here is one last illustration, a final story to help us embrace what the blood covenant really means for us.

In 1965, our country was embroiled in the Vietnam War. I was largely unaffected by the war until my dad, a career Air Force man, was deployed to Saigon. He would serve for two years before coming home. While he was there, he took on an additional challenge, holding great promise for us back home. My parents had three sons in a row. I was the baby and a wonderful child, but my mom nevertheless pined for a daughter. Thus began the conversation about adopting a Vietnamese national, a baby girl. Great effort was invested with the state department, the Air Force, and the governing officials of South Vietnam. It was an arduous process, but the Lord blessed us, and Dad was green-lighted to begin the daunting task of selecting baby girl Fyffe.

Finding available babies wasn't hard; they were everywhere. Orphaned children abounded, as did the orphanages. Dad spent weekends visiting orphanages and looking at who knows how many babies. But he finally found her. She was just over a year old. Her life had mostly been spent in a simple bassinet in front of an open window in a crowded orphanage. She wasn't well; she had bronchitis, was malnourished, and was oddly disproportioned. Her head was normal for her age, but her little body was about half the size it should have been, the result of not enough of anything needed. Frankly, there wasn't much of a reason to stop and consider her. There were so many little girls in better health; surely one of them would be a more attractive choice? But for Dad, there was just something about her—she was the one.

He found her when he approached her bassinet, and she managed to catch his attention. She smiled, cooed, and made eye contact. As sick as she was, she still had the spark and found the strength to look up; she noticed him. Well, *bam*, that did it. The search was over. The woman at the orphanage tried to change his mind; she pointed to healthier baby girls. But no, he had made his decision. The sickly little girl was named Tran Ti Kim Lai. The initial paperwork got done, and Dad took her to the base hospital where she was admitted immediately. She would stay there for some weeks, slowly responding but certainly improving.

Eventually the day arrived. Arrangements were made through friends who were rotating back to the States, and they brought my new baby sister home. Mom flew to San Francisco to greet them and to see her new daughter coming off the plane. She stood there at the gate, anxiously waiting, and then the moment arrived. Dad's friends walked up to her and placed her daughter into her arms. Welcome to America, kid! We changed her name from Tran Ti Kim Lai to Meri. I thought her old name sounded cool. That was fifty years ago. In every way possible, she was absorbed into our family. She had our name, ate our food, and lived in our house. Well, of course, she did; she was a Fyffe. She was one of us, one of the family. When she learned to talk, she talked like we did, with a Texas accent. She had three big brothers who watched out for her. She was home. Our family was blessed, and is still blessed, by her coming into our lives.

Sometimes I think about how close she came to dying at the orphanage, probably within a couple of months, and maybe sooner. My father saved her life. But it wouldn't have happened if he had not stopped to see her, to give her a chance. That poor kid needed a break. She deserved to be loved and to be in someone's family. She was saved because someone who cared chose to care for her.

Our Heavenly Father cared. He stepped up to save Abram and, through him, all the rest of us. We would have certainly died apart from God and without hope. His purpose was to save those who needed saving, but saving them would require a sacrifice. Someone had to step up and do what no one else could do, or would do. In the same way that my dad chose my sister, so God chose us—He chose me.

It was always in His mind to do so.

> Praise be to the God and Father of our Lord Jesus Christ, who has blessed us in the heavenly realms with every spiritual blessing in Christ. For he chose us in him before the creation of the world to be holy and blameless in his sight. In love he predestined us to be adopted as sons through Jesus Christ, in accordance with his pleasure and will, to the praise of his glorious grace, which he has freely given us in the One he loves. (Ephesians 1:3–6)

One afternoon, a priest blew a ram's horn from high on a wall. The Lamb of God was slain, and the covenant was fulfilled. And it made all the difference. Covenants must be kept. My daughter got her dog. The world got redemption.

3

Moses Gets the Water

How hard would it be to be in a desert without the essential resources needed to survive? Actually, it would be incredibly hard, and in many deserts, the likely result would be death. Someone once said, "If you want to die, then walk into the desert with nothing and keep walking until you collapse." Someone may be right. Most deserts are unsuitable for family camping. They aren't popular vacation destinations or the place for a charming three-day weekend. Deserts can be unbearably hot, decidedly dangerous, and certainly uninhabitable. In other words, they are deadly.

The Judean Desert is a harsh and unforgiving wilderness, offering triple-digit heat for several months of the year.[1] It provides little, if any, lifesaving elements. Only a fool would willingly go there without enough water, food, and whatever was needed to get out alive. Israel's southern deserts can be survived, but only by those who have learned to live there, namely the nomadic Bedouin. For the rest of us, better that we appreciate the Judean Desert by visiting its historical sites and landmarks and then drive back to civilization.

As ironic as it may be, the Judean Desert's austerity made it the perfect place to seek a deeper connection with God.[2] If you were in the desert, then you were vulnerable, with only your faith in God to help you. You would need to fully rely on Him because He was your only hope of getting out alive. That desert dynamic was true for one person, a group of people, or for an entire nation. It was true for Abraham, Isaac, Elijah, and for John the Baptist. It was true for Jesus during his forty days in the wilderness. And it was true for Moses, who, 3500 years ago, led a million plus people into the desert. What did Abraham, Moses, and all the others have in common? They all spent time in the desert, and they all had to fully rely on God to get out alive.

This chapter is about water. We will first explore how water affected Moses's life and his years in the desert. Next we will discover the role that water played in Jesus's teaching. We will see how Jesus fulfilled Ezekiel's vision of water trickling out of the temple and becoming a river of life flowing through the desert. And finally, we will establish the significance of water as a powerful picture of the Holy Spirit.

Let's now take a closer look at Moses in the desert. Perhaps we will learn more of how all this matters to us and how it helps us have a stronger connection with Jesus, our Messiah.

From the Hebrew Text

The Slaves of Egypt

Try to imagine all the generations of Hebrew slaves, each one living and dying under the yoke of slavery. Did they dream of the day when someone would give them deliverance? Were God's promises to Abraham becoming less real? After a few centuries, were they even aware of the promises? Was it increasingly difficult to teach their children about the God of Abraham, Isaac, and Jacob?

God told Abraham that his descendants would live in slavery for four hundred years (Genesis 15:13). Was there a Promise Land calendar passed through the generations, marking off the decades and centuries until the four hundredth year would arrive? Had God's promises to Abraham faded into the landscape of time and circumstance? In reading the Exodus story, it doesn't appear they were packing for the journey or getting organized to leave. But it was the four hundredth year, and it was time to go.

Moses: Prince and Shepherd

One day, an eighty-year-old man walked into Ramses. He had once lived there and had been a prince of Egypt, but there wasn't a cheering crowd to greet him. Moses didn't enter the city with the pomp and glory befitting royalty but in the quiet humility of a country shepherd. His reappearance and purpose were met with great opposition. It was an epic battle between Moses and Pharaoh, but in time, Moses prevailed. At long last, and exactly when the Lord had said, the Hebrew people were set free.

Moses led them into the desert and to Mount Sinai, where they entered a covenant with God. That covenant gave them a tangible connection, a sense of belonging, and a way to worship Him in holiness. The Ten Commandments and the Law of Moses gave them identity with Yahweh and an incentive to follow Moses.

Moses Leads Them to Canaan

Having completed all that was meant to happen at Sinai, they were finally ready. The journey wouldn't be easy; they would be confronted by the harsh realities of the desert. Before it was over, they would question the purpose of God and would doubt Moses as their leader.

Between the Hebrew nation and the Promise Land was a vast series of deserts, and crossing them was the only path forward. Moses led them, armed with the *staff*, a physical presence of God's authority and power (Exodus 4:17–20, Numbers 17). The staff had a key role to play in a life-changing moment for Moses. It would be about water.

The responsibility for the entire Hebrew nation rested on Moses's shoulders. Yes, it was really on the Lord's shoulders, but no doubt Moses still felt immense pressure. I'm guessing he found himself praying more often and with greater passion. The journey from Ramses to Sinai and then from Sinai to Jericho had a series of difficult challenges, some of which were the following:

1. Pharaoh changing his mind and pursuing them to bring them back

2. Trapped—the Red Sea in front and the Egyptians at their backs

3. Getting everyone across the Red Sea in a single night

4. Coming down from Mount Sinai to find rebellion, immorality, and idolatry

5. The pressure of providing daily for a million people and their animals

6. Dealing with the logistics for tents, sanitation, etc.

7. Water—how to get enough water for all those people and their animals

8. Coping with the constant grumbling, complaining, and doubting

One of their frequent complaints was, of course, about the lack of water. One of the occasions when they were grumbling was when they camped in the Desert of Zin. I've been to the Desert of Zin. I didn't camp there or face any of their challenges, but I was there long enough to know that it's desolate and uninhabitable. I didn't see a bird, an insect, or so much as a lizard. I'm not saying lizards and bugs weren't there, just that I didn't see any! The Israelites, probably a million plus people, along with their livestock, were very unhappy. Take a moment to read what the people said to Moses.

> In the first month the whole Israelite community arrived at the Desert of Zin, and they stayed at Kadesh. There Miriam died and was buried. Now there was no water for the community, and the people gathered in opposition to Moses and Aaron. They quarreled with Moses and said, "If only we had died when our brothers fell dead before the Lord! Why did you bring the Lord's community into this desert, that we and our livestock should die here? Why did you bring us up out of Egypt to this terrible place? It has no grain or figs, grapevines or pomegranates. And there is no water to drink!" (Numbers 20:1–5)

Nice attitude, huh? They were happy enough when they left Ramses with their freedom and pockets filled with gold. However, they still maintained a slave mentality. They were born into bondage, abused as slaves, and not in possession of a strong and abiding faith. At times, they neither trusted God nor had confidence in Moses, so they chose to complain, grumble, and doubt as they did in the Zin Desert. They were out of patience, not that they had yet demonstrated much patience. "We could have stayed in Egypt; at least there was food and water in Egypt" (Numbers 20:2–5).

I wonder if Moses was getting frustrated with them, for clearly, they were in the desert, but they were not yet fully relying on God.

Moses Gets the Water

How much water did the people and their herds require? They certainly needed a sustainable source for drinking, bathing, cleaning their clothes, and for everything else for which water is needed. The flocks and herds alone would require hundreds of thousands of gallons. They would need water for days, and possibly for weeks, for as long they camped at Kadesh.

To address the water issue, God told Moses to take the staff and speak to the rock, and from the rock water would flow. Let's pause for a moment and think about this "rock." For a long time, I imagined Moses speaking to some randomly selected, relatively small rock on the desert floor. I imagined it being the size of a bowling ball. But I no longer think so. The Hebrew word for *rock* used in Numbers 20:8 is *seh'-lah*, a Hebrew root which defined "to be lofty; a craggy rock, literally or figuratively (a fortress): a (ragged rock), or stony strong hold."

Does that word suggest a rock the size of a bowling ball or a small boulder? The Israelite camp didn't need a trickle of water seeping out of a small stone, or even from a boulder putting out hundreds of gallons of water. The people's needs far exceeded those relatively small sources, even if the water was miraculously provided. The rock must have been much larger, something from which millions of gallons could flow.

In the Desert of Zin is a canyon cut deep into a huge mountain. It can be seen for miles. I've hiked that canyon. Start walking, and in a few minutes, there are signs of damp ground, nothing much, only what a trickle of water would leave on a patch of parched dirt. Keep walking. A little farther, and the ground becomes a rocky creek bed. Hike a little more, and suddenly, there flows a small stream. Continue, and the stream becomes wider and deeper. Eventually you reach the head of the canyon, and there, gushing out of the face of a massive rock wall, is a waterfall. It creates a large pool , out from which flows the river that slowly dries up as it reaches the mouth of the canyon. This rock, or canyon wall, is the traditional site believed to be where Moses got the water. The tradition also holds that the water continues to pour because Moses never stopped it. The water was a gift from God, for water meant life, and that water literally saved their lives.

Moses was told to speak to the rock, but we know that he didn't. He hit it with the staff, twice. Even though Moses disobeyed God, the power of the staff still created the river. It was a beautiful blessing for the people but was a crisis moment for Moses. He got the water, but he disobeyed the Lord. With apparent anger, he hit the canyon wall, perhaps like a slugger with a bat, and he used the holy staff of God to do it, and he did so in front of the whole community.

On to the Promise Land

From Kadesh, Moses led them to the edge of the Promise Land. The twelve spies were sent into Canaan, one from each tribe, to explore and survey the land. What was their report? That it truly was flowing with milk and honey. But most of the spies feared that they and their families would be slaughtered if they entered the land. Imagine, all that way from Ramses only to stop at the one-yard line. Their choice to not enter the Promise Land had terrible consequences. They were sentenced to wander the desert for forty years, one year for each day the spies were in the land (Numbers 14:34). All the people ages twenty and up would die in the desert, their hopes and dreams dying with them (Numbers 14:29). Year after year, Moses could do nothing else but lead them from place to place, watching them die their meaningless deaths. It must have been excruciating. Finally, when the last person of that last generation died, Moses could then take Abraham's descendants to the Promise Land.

What Happened to Moses?

Did Moses get to enter Canaan with its wealth of orchards, vineyards, and fields of grain? Did he get first choice of a beautiful farm with a fine house in the green hills of Galilee? No, he didn't. The Lord brought him to Mount Nebo on top of Pisgah on the east side of the Jordan River. There, he had a full view of the Promise Land that he led the people to inherit, but there was no inheritance for Moses.

Moses died while living in Moab, within sight of the Promise Land, but he never touched it. What happened? Why did God prevent him from entering? In that moment back in the Desert of Zin, Moses made a massive mistake. He failed to demonstrate God as holy, disrespecting Him by striking the rock, and he did it in front of the people (Numbers 20:11). As a consequence, God kept him out of Canaan. It was a severe penalty for a serious mistake. With heart-stabbing, gut-wrenching irony, Moses was banned from entering because he sinned while getting the water for the people.

Moses was God's choice for bringing Abraham's descendants out of captivity. He got the water, for without it, the people would have perished and Israel would have failed.

His story brings into clarity the need for Jesus, our Messiah. Consider all the Lord did for Moses and Israel. God provided Moses with his brother, Aaron, because Moses doubted his own communication skills. He gave Moses the staff of power, enabling him to perform the miraculous signs. He divided the waters of the Red Sea and then destroyed their enemy as they attempted to cross. God entered into a covenant with them, making them His chosen nation. He gave them the law. He provided for them in the desert. Yet with all of that, Moses still disobeyed, the people were still faithless, and none of them could keep the law. Even with the staff of power, Moses still failed.

In all of that, God was showing the people that He loved them and that His desire was to care and provide for them. However, God didn't provide the water, the covenant, and the staff of power because the people were perfect. He kept them safe and even kept their clothes from wearing out, but not because they deserved it. He provided all those things so the imperfect people would understand that God was perfect and that He was gracious and loving.

The Lord was also establishing that the people couldn't walk blamelessly before him because they weren't blameless people. They were imperfect, broken, and sinful. They couldn't keep the law, and as far as that goes, neither could we.

Like the Israelites in the desert, we know what it is to thirst, but we need a different kind of water. And we need it to flow through a different kind of covenant. The new and better covenant comes through Jesus, our Messiah.

On the day of God's choosing, Jesus stood in for us and was sacrificed. He was the righteous substitute for our sins when God fulfilled the blood covenant.

We look to Jesus of Nazareth and the Living Water.

From the Greek Text

There are some interesting similarities between Moses and Jesus. The birth of Moses and his adoption by Pharaoh's daughter saved his life. The Messiah's birth generated Herod's attention, which forced Mary and Joseph to take him to Egypt to save his life. The miracles Moses performed resulted in the people having faith. The miraculous signs Jesus performed resulted in people having faith. After their oldest sons were killed, the Egyptians set the Israelites free. After God's Son was killed, the people were set free. It was the lambs' blood on the doorposts that would spare the Hebrews' firstborn sons. It was the blood of the Lamb that spared all of us. Moses brought the water to sustain the lives of his people. Jesus brought the water of life to sustain the souls of mankind.

Jesus and Water

Jesus, of course, understood that water was a powerful symbol of the Holy Spirit. He understood how water symbolized God's blessings for the people. For them, water was life.

Jesus lived in an agrarian culture. Although he wasn't raised to be a farmer, he still was familiar with the crops, orchards, and vineyards, and with fishing. There was abundant water there, and the Sea of Galilee was just seventeen miles east of Nazareth.

Jesus often used water in his teaching and ministry. He gathered people on the shore of the Sea of Galilee to preach to them. He used Peter's fishing boat as a floating pulpit. He took Peter and Andrew into deeper water for a miraculous catch. He used a fish with a coin in its mouth to teach a lesson to Peter. He walked on water, and he calmed the windswept waves on the Sea of Galilee. Here are some examples of how Jesus used water in his ministry:

- He changed water to wine (John 2:1–11).

- He and his disciples were baptized in the Jordan (John 3:22).

- He offered a Samaritan woman Living Water (John 4:1–13).

- He healed the lame man at the Pool of Bethesda (John 5:1–9).

- He walked on water at the Sea of Galilee (John 6:16–20).

Jesus at the Feast of Tabernacles: The Living Water

One of Jesus's greatest teachings that utilized the symbol of water was given while he was at the Feast of Tabernacles. This feast was joyous for the Jews because it celebrated the intake of the harvest. They worshiped God for their crops and orchards and for being able to feed their families and their nation. God gave the water, and the water created life. This feast also remembered how God had provided for their ancestors while crossing the desert, leaving Egypt for the Promise Land.

We read in John 7 that Jesus was there at the temple during the Feast of Tabernacles. It was within the context of water, the harvest, and divine providence that he stood up to speak and said something amazing. Let's take a brief look at what was happening that led up to that moment.

Tabernacles[3] began each morning with a processional from the temple to the Pool of Siloam. A priest carried an empty golden pitcher and led the worshipers to the pool while they sang songs of great joy. The worshipers carried branches in each hand, the etrog and the lulav.[4] They were cut from trees listed in Leviticus 23:39–43. The branches represented the trees their ancestors encountered on their journey to Canaan and those they inherited in the Promise Land. It was a tremendously strong and meaningful experience, praising and thanking God for all His gifts and blessings. The worshipers shook them at certain moments, relating to the songs they were singing.

At the Pool of Siloam, the priest filled the pitcher with water, and then he led the worshipers back to the temple, continuing their joyful songs. At the temple, the priest lifted the golden pitcher and poured the water on the altar. It was a sacrifice of praise, for without the water that God provided, nothing could grow, no food would exist, and Israel would fail.

At the Feast of Tabernacles, within the context of the water being poured on the altar, Jesus made a reference to a river of living water (John 7:38). I believe he was referring to Ezekiel 47, and perhaps to the many OT references of water as blessing from God for life. Jesus was about to fulfill, or promise to fulfill, Ezekiel's vision of a great river of living water. Let's look at Ezekiel's vision.

> And I saw water coming out from under the threshold of the temple toward the east for the temple faced east. He then brought me out through the north gate and led me around the outside to the outer gate facing

east, and the water was flowing from the south side. He measured off another thousand, (cubits) but now it was a river that I could not cross, because the water had risen and was deep enough to swim in—a river that no one could cross.[6] He asked me, "Son of man, do you see this?" Then he led me back to the bank of the river.[7] When I arrived there, I saw a great number of trees on each side of the river.[8] He said to me, "This water flows toward the eastern region and goes down into the Arabah, where it enters the Dead Sea. When it empties into the sea, the salty water there becomes fresh.[9] Swarms of living creatures will live wherever the river flows. There will be large numbers of fish, because this water flows there and makes the salt water fresh; so where the river flows everything will live.[10] Fishermen will stand along the shore; from En Gedi to En Eglaim there will be places for spreading nets. The fish will be of many kinds—like the fish of the Mediterranean Sea.[11] But the swamps and marshes will not become fresh; they will be left for salt.[12] Fruit trees of all kinds will grow on both banks of the river. Their leaves will not wither, nor will their fruit fail. Every month they will bear fruit, because the water from the sanctuary flows to them. Their fruit will serve for food and their leaves for healing. (Ezekiel 47:1–2, 5–12)

Ezekiel's vision of the river of living water painted a picture of trees in season all year long. The river had power to transform saltwater into fresh. It contained many kinds of fish, like the Mediterranean Sea. It was a river that gave and sustained life. It transformed everything it touched and brought renewal, revival, and restoration. I believe that Jesus's teaching on "rivers of flowing water" was based on Ezekiel's vision.

Jesus was there that day at the Feast of Tabernacles and probably participated in the morning celebrations. Jesus understood Ezekiel's vision. From that historical and prophetic background, Jesus offered life-giving water to whoever was thirsty.

> On the last and greatest day of the festival, Jesus stood and said in a loud voice, "Let anyone who is thirsty come to me and drink.[38] Whoever believes in me, as Scripture has said, rivers of living water will flow from within them." By this he meant the Spirit, whom those who believed in him were later to receive. Up to that time the Spirit had not been given, since Jesus had not yet been glorified. (John 7:37–39)[37]

On the last and greatest day of the festival, the priest with the pitcher of water walked around the altar seven times, then poured it out. The final day of the festival culminated the entire celebration year. It was the last day, the final day, of all the feasts for that year.

This transformational power of the Holy Spirit was portrayed in Ezekiel's vision of the river, the water flowing from the sanctuary. Jesus fulfilled Ezekiel's prophecy by offering them the promised Holy Spirit, a unique and beautiful gift for all who believed.

The Water

The water Moses got from the rock became shallower as it flowed and eventually dried up. Ezekiel's river was shallow where it started but got deeper as it flowed. Moses got the water essential for survival, but it was temporary, and it didn't flow with them when they left the Desert of Zin. But Ezekiel's river, becoming deeper and wider as it flowed, provided life and renewal in boundless supply. The law was limited; it couldn't really cleanse the worshiper. The Spirit sets us free, and is within us; it flows through us as we joyously celebrate the victory.

Moses produced life-sustaining water in the desert. Ezekiel promised a flowing river of transformation. Jesus provided salvation through the Living Water.

Moses got the water. Ezekiel saw a river. Jesus gave the Spirit.

For Us Today

In the summer between my seventh and eighth grades, a nice lady at church offered me a job. She needed someone to care of her yard while they were on vacation for two weeks. I said yes. She invited me over to show me around and explain everything. I thought to myself, *Explain everything? What was there to explain? It's a yard. Turn on the hose and water the grass, no big deal.*

It was a big deal. Her "yard" was huge. Not only was there a lot of grass, but she also had all kinds of trees, a vegetable garden, flower beds, shrubs, and climbing vines. This was Arizona in July, and it was blistering hot. Most of us had yards of rocks and cactus. But not her. Her yard was an oasis, and it needed a lot of water, and automatic sprinkler systems were years away. This was about Ricky getting the water.

As we walked around, she explained in great detail how to water everything. The lawn got watered on certain days, using the front and back hoses. The vegetable garden, flower beds, bushes, and shrubs all got certain amounts of water. Some things got watered daily; some, every other day. If done correctly, she told me, the job would take two to three hours each day. This seemed like a lot of trouble, but I had agreed to do it; and there was, after all, a pot of gold at the end.

So they left on vacation assured that Ricky had everything under control. Well, I did great. I was conscientious and applied myself to the task. But after a few days, it got a little dull and boring. Besides, it was hot, so I began to take some shortcuts. Funny that it didn't occur to me that taking shortcuts to beat the heat meant less water on the green things. Oh well, back to the shortcuts. Surely the shrubs could get by with five minutes instead of seven. Surely the grass didn't need to be watered as much as she said—and so forth. You get the idea?

The two weeks ended, the family came home, and I was summoned. I got there quickly and happily rang the doorbell, expecting a pat on the back and some hard-earned cash. She opened the door, stepped out, and once again, walked me around to look at the yard. Over the two weeks, some of the grass had gotten crusty. Some of the flowers were drooping sadly. There were plants in the vegetable garden that were turning brown, and they weren't supposed to turn brown.

She asked, "Ricky, were you careful to water everything just as I explained to you?" I answered, "Uh, yes, ma'am, sort of." She said, "What does 'sort of' mean?" I said, "Well, you know…" She wasn't very happy with me. My careless approach to caring for her yard put living things in distress. Some of her lovely things just weren't anymore. Some were on their way out, and some were just out. To this day, I remember the look on her face.

Sometimes I wonder what opportunities or blessings I've missed due to my own disobedience, like Moses with the rock. Moses reminds us that we should be grateful for a covenant where sins are forgiven, souls are restored, and all is made new by the Living Water of God's Spirit.

A final thought about the lady and her yard—even though I let her down by not keeping my word, she still paid me, all of it. She didn't have to, but the truth is, she loved me. She was my Sunday morning Bible class teacher and was committed to my becoming a godly young man. It was a lovely gift of grace from a beautiful and godly woman. Moses got the water so Israel could survive, but he was banished from entering Canaan.

Jesus offered living water to the woman at the well, and then to her village, and then to all who believed. Ezekiel's river of living water came from the sanctuary, that divine and holy place that brings us in and makes us whole, filling us with the Holy Spirit.

Like that yard in the Arizona desert, we also depend on the water, or we too will begin to sag and sadly droop and become less lovely.

Jesus answered her, "If you knew the gift of God and who it is that asks you for a drink, you would have asked him and he would have given you living water" (John 4:10).

4

The Messiah's Seven Feasts

Like millions of other children, I loved the holidays. The thoughts of Christmas were always very exciting to me. I liked the lights on the tree and the decorations on the house, the homemade candy from Grandma, and of course, the presents. Having brightly wrapped packages with my name on them—I mean, *wow*! Christmas was magical. Then there was Thanksgiving, the Fourth of July, Halloween with the candy, Presidents' Day, New Year's Eve? Well, I loved the holidays. It would be some years before realizing Halloween wasn't really a holiday, but I didn't care.

In our family, the holidays were largely about Dad being off work, us kids being out of school, and Mom cooking a lot of really fabulous food. As I got older, the significance of the holidays became more important, more meaningful. However, my holiday experiences were very different from those of other cultures, especially the Jews living under the Law of Moses. They had seven major feasts each year, and none of them were anything like I experienced as a child. Most of our annual observances are not of a religious nature. Christmas and Easter share the thread of Jesus's birth and resurrection, but many Americans do not celebrate these holidays in any religious sense but view them as a secular or cultural event.

Our holidays don't require personal preparations of the mind, heart, and soul. Ours are also mostly independent of one another: The Fourth of July has nothing to do with Thanksgiving. New Year's Eve has nothing in common with Washington's birthday. The Jewish feasts were not like our holidays, so it may be challenging for Western Gentiles to relate to the seven feasts. For they all interconnect, require a significant amount of personal preparation, and are deeply spiritual in nature.

The Celebration Calendar of the Seven Jewish Feasts

It doesn't take long to get a little confused about the Jewish feasts. Although they are fascinating and filled with rich theology, they can, at times, be a bit hard to grasp. But they are so worth the effort. The feasts all interconnect with one another and weave a beautiful tapestry of the Jewish history with God and His people.

There were seven major feasts that occurred on the Jewish celebration calendar.[1] The Jews maintained two calendars: the lunar and the celebration calendar. The former tracked the months and seasons of the year; the latter scheduled the celebratory feasts. Some feasts were observed in a single day while others took place over an entire week. The single-day observances often marked the beginning of the weeklong celebrations.

The feasts told the stories of Yahweh's power, salvation, and providential care. They were annual reminders of His promises to Abraham and his descendants. Through these celebrations, the Jews remained connected to God and to one another. The feasts helped keep the people rooted in the faith, sustaining their heritage of faith and dependence upon their Adonai.

The Jewish Feasts and the Messiah

The feasts can seem opaque, making it harder to get a grasp on their meaning and purpose. They were rooted in the Law of Moses, and unpacking their significance requires a commitment to the Hebrew text. As we read about and study the feasts, some questions begin to formulate:

- Are the feasts mentioned in the Gospels?
- Does Jesus connect with his own heritage in regard to the feasts?
- Does Paul or any other NT writer mention them?

These are significant questions, and their answers are equally so. Actually, much of Jesus's ministry took place in and around the feasts. From childhood to the cross, his life and ministry were deeply affected by, and deeply connected to, the Jewish feasts. He didn't ignore them; he observed them, making the journeys to Jerusalem to participate in their observances. I believe they meant a great deal to him not just because of heritage but because the feasts themselves were so immersed in messianic purpose. Jesus would never be disrespectful or show dishonor to Torah. As we know, he was committed to not breaking even the least of the commandments.

> Do not think that I have come to abolish the Law or the Prophets; I have not come to abolish them but to fulfill them. For truly I tell you, until heaven and earth disappear, not the smallest letter, not the least stroke of a pen, will by any means disappear from the Law until everything is accomplished. (Matthew 5:17–18)

So wouldn't this text bind him to observe the feasts? Is there evidence of his doing so? Beyond the immediate significance to the Jews living under the law, might there also be a greater purpose to the feasts? Ultimately, were they instituted to lead the world to the coming Messiah, to a brighter and better covenant? Certainly each celebration had deep spiritual, cultural, and historical meaning to the people. But they also painted a picture of the messianic kingdom. As we look more closely at Jesus, we may discover a greater significance in the feasts. Likewise, if we better understand the feasts, it may well move us forward and closer to Jesus. Let's see what we can discover as we take a look at each of the seven feasts.

The Hebrew word for *feast* is *moadim*, which, when translated, means "appointed times." Jewish males were required to observe three annual feasts in Jerusalem at their appointed times (see Deuteronomy 1:6).

A good text to begin with is Leviticus 23. Perhaps this text, more than any other, provides the clearest listing and explanation of each feast. In the order of their occurrence, they are the following:

1. Feast of Passover

2. Feast of Unleavened Bread

3. Feast of Firstfruits

4. Festival of Weeks

5. Festival of Trumpets

6. Day of Atonement

7. Festival of Tabernacles

The First Feast: Passover or Pesach[2]

From the Hebrew Text

The festival year began with the observance of Passover, which took place on the fifteenth day of Nisan, the first month of the celebration calendar. This feast was known as the feast of salvation. It had its origin in Egypt when God sent the destroying angel to kill the firstborn son of each home (Exodus 11–12). For those who had applied lamb's blood to their doorframes, the angel passed over, sparing or saving the firstborn son. The Egyptians, of course, unaware of the power of the lamb's blood, suffered a night of terrible grief in their homes. After this tenth and final plague, Pharaoh finally relented; and the Hebrew people, some six hundred thousand men and their families, were not only released but also sent out with gold, flocks and herds, and possessions.

Passover was the feast celebrating salvation. On the evening of Passover, the people gathered in their homes and shared a meal, a meal prepared and eaten in "haste," for they would soon be leaving Egypt. The menu was as follows:

- Roasted lamb
- Unleavened bread (there was no time for yeast to rise)
- Bitter herbs (to remind them of the bitterness of captivity)

The people ate the meal while standing, and they were dressed for the journey.

From the Greek Text

That first Passover in Egypt demonstrated God's commitment to His people. During the night, He provided an escape, a door of salvation. If they would apply the lamb's blood upon their doorframes, then death would pass over their homes, sparing their firstborn sons. Much later, God would choose not to pass over His "firstborn Son" but instead sacrifice him so all are spared, and his blood saved all.

The Parallels between Passover and Calvary

- The lamb's blood on the doorposts; the Lamb of God who takes away our sin

- Leave pagan Egypt behind; live the new life, renewed and restored to God

- Liberated from slavery; set free from our bondage of sin

- Spared death by the blood of the lamb; given life by the blood of Christ

- A memorial meal shared together; the Lord's supper shared among believers

Each family made careful preparations in anticipation of Passover. Much effort was made to remove all leaven from their homes. The lamb had to be selected, the meal prepared, and there were other preparations to make as well.[3]

It suggests one obvious question: How do we prepare our hearts for worship, to share in his meal, to honor his sacrifice, since Jesus is our Passover Lamb?

Look, the Lamb of God who takes away the sin of the
world. (John 1:29)

Get rid of the old yeast that you may be a new batch
without yeast, as your really are. For Christ, our
Passover lamb has been sacrificed. (1 Corinthians 5:7)

The Messiah's Seven Feasts

Feast	Jewish purpose	Messianic fulfillment
Passover (Pesach)	Celebrate salvation	Jesus is our Passover Lamb.

The Second Feast: Unleavened Bread or Chag HaMotzi

From the Hebrew Text

The Feast of Unleavened Bread was a seven-day observance
and addressed the theme of purity. The first day of the feast
was Passover, held on Nisan 15. Then Passover was followed
by six more days of eating unleavened bread. As the people
readied themselves and their homes for the celebration of
Passover and Unleavened Bread, they purged all the leaven
from their houses. They collected the leaven and then
burned it in the leaven package. This was done on Nisan
14, the day before Passover. Bread without yeast suggested
a couple of ideas:

- The people were to eat in haste, being ready to leave,
  so there was no time for the dough to rise.

- Leaven or yeast in scripture was often a symbol for
  sin and unbelief.

This purification was about physically removing the leaven—and symbolically, the sin—from their lives and homes. Having done so, they were spiritually and physically prepared to celebrate the Passover and the Feast of Unleavened Bread.

From the Greek Text

Consider these verses:

- "'Be careful,' Jesus said to them. 'Be on your guard against the yeast of the Pharisees and Sadducees'" (Matthew 16:6).[4]

- "Then they understood that he was not telling them to guard against the yeast used in bread, but against the teaching of the Pharisees and Sadducees" (Matthew 16:12).

- "Therefore let us keep the Festival, not with the old yeast, the yeast of malice and wickedness, but with bread without yeast, the bread of sincerity and truth" (1 Corinthians 5:8).

Eating unleavened bread symbolized a holy walk with God.[5] This was about personal purity, removing the sin from minds and hearts, a process of personal introspection. Each worshiper might ask, *Is there anything in my life that needs to be repented of and purged before Passover and Unleavened Bread?*

Consider these parallels between Jesus and the Feast of Unleavened Bread:

1. Jesus was crucified on Nisan 14.

   - This was the day leaven was burned in the Jewish homes as a symbol of purging sin and evil.

- Jesus was crucified on Nisan 14 to remove sin and evil from our lives.

2. Bread is a common commodity in scripture and mentioned often.

- Food was provided in the desert as manna, a wafer made from coriander seed, which tasted sweet like honey.

- Bread as a symbol of the Messiah.

  ○ It was prophesied that his coming would bless the land with rain, fertility, and abundance (see Joel 2:12–32, 3:13–18).

  ○ Jesus is represented as the Bread of Life (John 6:35).

  ○ Jesus was born in Bethlehem—or, in Hebrew, *Beth Laheim*, meaning "the house or place of bread."

  ○ The newborn Messiah was laid in a manger, which was a hewn-out trough in the stone floor where grain was poured for animals to eat.

  ○ When Jesus was on the road to Emmaus, speaking with some disciples, they arrived at a village and shared a meal together, where Jesus broke bread and gave it to them. After eating the bread, their eyes were opened to see him (Luke 24:13–35)—the bread of sincerity and truth!

  ○ Today many believers worldwide share unleavened bread together in the communion meal. Jesus, the Bread of Life.

The Messiah's Seven Feasts

Feast	Jewish purpose	Messianic fulfillment
Passover (Pesach)	Celebrate salvation	Jesus is our Passover Lamb.
Unleavened Bread (Chag HaMotzi)	Personal purity before God	Jesus purifies us from sin.

The Third Feast: Firstfruits or Reishit Katzir

From the Hebrew Text

The celebration of Firstfruits began at the end of Unleavened Bread, on the morning after the Sabbath. This feast was dedicated to honoring God for the fertility of the land, the crops, and the harvest. Passover remembered the night of salvation in Egypt; and Unleavened Bread, the purging of sin that hindered progress with God. Firstfruits was about Canaan, the land of milk and honey, the land God promised to Abraham and his descendants (Exodus 33:1–3). It was the land Joshua led the Israelites to inherit after conquering the seven pagan nations, also known as the land of the seven (Joshua 3).

On the day of Firstfruits, the people came with an offering from their early spring crops to "wave the sheaf" before the Lord. This festival wasn't just about fertile soil but about God replanting the earth in the spring.

From the Greek Text

The modern church refers to the Feast of Firstfruits as Easter, the resurrection day of Christ. The origins of Easter are mostly pagan in nature and are based on Ishtar, the goddess of fertility.[6] Today some Christians equate Easter with an egg hunt and a cute, fuzzy large rabbit. Some Christians have perhaps never wondered why a large bunny with a basket of colored eggs reflects the glory of the Risen Savior. The answer, of course, is that the bunny and eggs have nothing to do with the Messiah's resurrection. The rabbit and eggs are symbols of fertility and also originate from pagan fertility rites. It's not difficult to see how it was fused in with the resurrection, new life, being born again, a new creation, etc.

For us, the Feast of Firstfruits is the resurrection feast, corresponding to the day that Jesus was raised from the dead. The text refers to Jesus being the firstfruits from the dead.

- "That the Messiah would suffer and, as the first to rise from the dead, would bring the message of light to his own people and to the Gentiles" (Acts 26:23).

- "The Son is the image of the invisible God, the firstborn over all creation" (Colossians 1:15).

- "And he is the head of the body, the church; he is the beginning and the firstborn from among the dead, so that in everything he might have the supremacy" (Colossians 1:18).

- "But each in turn: Christ, the first fruits; then, when he comes, those who belong to him" (1 Corinthians 15:23).

The Messiah's Seven Feasts

Feast	Jewish purpose	Messianic fulfillment
Passover (Pesach)	Celebrate salvation	Jesus is our Passover Lamb.
Unleavened Bread (Chag HaMotzi)	Personal purity before God	Jesus purifies us from sin.
Firstfruits (Reishit Katzir)	Celebration of new life	Jesus is first from the dead.

The Fourth Feast: Weeks, Pentecost, or Shavout

From the Hebrew Text

Pentecost means "fifty" in Greek. The Day of Pentecost, or Shavuot in Hebrew, recognized the fiftieth day from their Hebrew ancestors leaving Egypt and arriving at Mount Sinai. This feast celebrated Moses receiving the Ten Commandments. Shavuot was also known as the conclusion of Passover, the night that the lamb's blood spared their firstborn sons. Passover also symbolized the beginning of the Hebrews' pursuit of the Promised Land. Their pursuit really began after they received the law and entered into the Sinai covenant fifty days after leaving Ramses.

God, through Moses, separated His people from the pagans. They came out from them and were made holy (Leviticus 11:44–45, 20:26; Deuteronomy 7:6). The covenant made between Yahweh and Israel centered on their becoming a nation of God's own possession, His treasured possession. They were unique. From among all the nations of the earth, Yahweh entered into a covenant with the descendants of Abraham.

From the Greek Text

Jesus declared to his disciples in Matthew 16 that he would build his church. It's an interesting word, *church*—not easily identified in the Greek New Testament with how the word is used in our common vocabulary. Jesus used a word that would better indicate the gathering of his *talmadim* or his disciples. Jesus didn't erect a series of buildings and structures in which to host worship services. Nor did he endeavor to create a denomination defined and identified as a hybrid between scripture and the creeds, practices, and traditions of men. His purpose was to build a holy temple, a kingdom of conscience, so people could exist together in sacred harmony, in holy community, and as vessels of the Spirit.

In the Messiah's kingdom, Pentecost or Shavuot, was the day when the Holy Spirit was poured out on all mankind (Joel 2 and Acts 2). Pentecost is the beginning of a better covenant, a relationship with the Messiah in holy and sanctified community, a community purposed for the praise and glory of the King of kings and Lord of lords, the head of the church. As Peter said in his first letter,

> But you are a chosen people, a royal priesthood, a holy nation, a people belonging to God, that you may declare the praises of him who called you out of darkness into his wonderful light. Once you were not a people, but now you are the people of God; once you had not received mercy, but now you have received mercy. (1 Peter 2:9–10)

The Messiah's Seven Feasts

Feast	Jewish purpose	Messianic fulfillment
Passover (Pesach)	Celebrate salvation	Jesus is our Passover Lamb.
Unleavened Bread (Hag HaMotzi)	Personal purity before God	Jesus purifies us from sin.
Firstfruits (Reishit Katzir)	Celebration of new life	Jesus is first from the dead.
Weeks (Shavuot)	Fifty days to Sinai (law)	Fifty days to Pentecost and the Holy Spirit

The Fifth Feast: Trumpets or Yom Teru'ah

From the Hebrew Text

The Feast of Trumpets took place on the first day of Tishri, or our September, and was established in Leviticus 23:24. Tishri was the seventh month on the lunar calendar, but it marked the end of the religious celebration calendar. The last three annual feasts took place in the month of Tishri:

- First day: Trumpets
- Tenth day: Atonement
- Seventeenth day: Tabernacles

Although the text doesn't specifically name the instrument used, tradition holds that it was the curved ram's horn, the shofar. Trumpets had a unique aspect in that no explanation was given for blowing the shofar. The feast was known as the day of blowing and was also known as the Festival of the Shofar.[7]

The Feast of Trumpets was not connected to any historical events in Israel, yet another unique aspect of this feast. Trumpets marked the beginning of a ten-day spiritual introspection. It was ten days of acknowledging sin, of repentance, and of seeking God's mercy before the execution of judgment on the Day of Atonement.

The Feast of Trumpets was focused on seeking God's forgiveness and cleansing, on getting right with Him. It wasn't a loud celebration but a quiet, thoughtful exploration of one's moral and spiritual life before God. In his book, Rabbi Lehrman writes,

> The Bible, which usually gives the reason for every observance, does not do so in the case of Rosh Hashanah (New Year or Feast of Trumpets), deeming the spiritual well-being of each individual too obvious to require comment. To subsequent teachers we owe the picture of a Day of Judgment on which all mortals pass before the Heavenly Throne to give an account of their deeds and to receive the promise of mercy.[8]

The blowing of the shofar was acknowledged as a call to repentance. It signified a time to prepare one's heart to stand trial before Yahweh on the Day of Atonement.

The Shofar: A Symbol of the Coming Messiah

- "And in that day a great trumpet will sound. Those who were perishing in Assyria and those who were exiled in Egypt will come and worship the Lord on the holy mountain in Jerusalem" (Isaiah 27:13).

- "Then the Lord will appear over them; his arrow will flash like lightning. The Sovereign Lord will sound the trumpet; he will march in the storms of the south" (Zechariah 9:14).

From the Greek Text

The sounding of the shofar not only announced the coming Messiah but also his second and final coming.

> "For the Lord himself will come down from heaven, with a loud command, with the voice of the archangel and with trumpet call of God, and the dead in Christ will rise first" (1 Thessalonians 4:16).

> "Listen, I tell you a mystery: We will not all sleep but we all be changed, in a flash, in the twinkling of an eye, at the last trumpet. For the trumpet will sound, the dead will be raised imperishable, and we will be changed" (1Corinthians 15:51–52).

The shofar was a sign, a symbol of divine mercy and forgiveness. The blowing of the shofar on the first day of Tishri reminded the people that they had ten days to seek forgiveness and mercy, cleansing and pardon. Philip Goodman wrote,

> Motivated by a profound faith in God's mercy and loving-kindness, the Jew renders an accounting of his life and actions during the past year before the Supreme Judge. But he does so with a feeling and ardent hope that the Almighty will pardon his shortcomings and gratify his yearning for spiritual regeneration.[9]

As Moses served as the deliverer of God's people from Egypt, so Jesus served to deliver us from the bondage of sin and death. The Feast of Trumpets called the faithful to repentance before the great and final judgment of God. But it was not a call to dread and fear but to rely on the grace and mercy of our Lord. In humbling ourselves before His almighty hand, we beseech His marvelous cleansing and His fabulous forgiveness!

This feast is perhaps the most Christ-centered of all. The Shofar announced a time of mercy and compassion. It symbolized the day of the Messiah and the everlasting mercy and compassion he brought in the New Covenant.

> But because of his great love for us, God, who is rich in mercy, made us alive with Christ even when we were dead in transgressions, it is by grace you have been saved. And God raised us up with Christ and seated us with him in the heavenly realms in Christ Jesus, in order that in the coming ages he might show the incomparable riches of his grace, expressed in his kindness to us in Christ Jesus. (Ephesians 2:4–7)

The Messiah's Seven Feasts

Feast	Jewish purpose	Messianic fulfillment
Passover (Pesach)	Celebrate salvation	Jesus is our Passover Lamb.
Unleavened Bread (Hag HaMotzi)	Personal purity before God	Jesus purifies us from sin.
Firstfruits (Reishit Katzir)	Celebration of new life	Jesus is first from the dead.
Weeks (Shavuot)	Fifty days to Sinai (law)	Fifty days to Pentecost and Holy Spirit
Trumpets (Yom Teru'ah)	Confession and mercy	Confession and grace

Richard N. Fyffe

The Sixth Feast: Atonement or Yom Kippur

From the Hebrew Text

The Great Day of Atonement, or Yom Kippur, was held on the tenth day of Tishri and represented the highest and most solemn of the holy days. It was the day all Israel could seek a new beginning, to obtain cleansing and forgiveness; it was a day of spiritual regeneration.

> Because on this day atonement will be made for you, to cleanse you. Then, before the Lord you will be clean from all your sins. (Leviticus 16:30)

Traditionally, the Jews believe that Adam was created on this day. So the Day of Atonement acknowledged both the creation of man as well as his need for renewed spiritual regeneration, provided through forgiveness. Naphtali Winter writes, "Man, the pinnacle of God's Creation, for whom everything else was created, stands newly created after having received atonement."[10]

Scripture calls it *Shabbat Shabbaton*, or the Sabbath of Sabbaths (Leviticus 16:31). In Hebrew, it's written as *Yom Ha-Kippurim*, a plural form suggesting that atonement was made for the many sins of the people. Yom Kippur was a day of confession and seeking atonement. The Hebrew root word for *kippur* is *kafar*, which means "ransom," a parallel word for *redeem* or *redemption*. This feast was preceded by ten days of repentance as signaled by the blowing of the shofar and the Feast of Trumpets. Rabbi Irving Greenberg writes,

> On Yom Kippur, the ritual trial reaches its conclusion... the people finally drop all their defenses and excuses and throw themselves on the mercy of the court, yet the same people never lose the conviction that they

will be pardoned. This atonement is by divine grace; it is above and beyond the individual effort or merit.[11]

The Day of Atonement was a day busy with sacrifices. Through the day, the high priest would sacrifice a bull and two male goats. One was sacrificed, and one was to be released as the scapegoat. The bull and goat's blood would be sprinkled on the curtain and on the horns of the altar to cleanse and sanctify them. It was a long and arduous day and fully relied on the high priest to make sacrifices for himself, his family, and for the people of Israel—and to do so in a perfect manner. Yet the high priest was only an imperfect man, sacrificing first for his own sins. The people needed a better covenant and a better high priest.

Yom Kippur demonstrated the beauty and power of the coming Messiah. He would apply blood to the cleansing and sanctifying of the people, his own.

From the Greek Text

Yom Kippur was a feast that began with a sinful man sacrificing animals for sinful men. But the Great Day of Atonement would ultimately end with Jesus of Nazareth, our Redeemer. He was the perfect sacrifice. By his wounds were the people healed. He served as a sinless high priest and as the perfect sacrifice.

> No man can redeem the life of another or give to God a ransom for him. The ransom for a life is costly, no payment is ever enough, that he should live on forever and not see decay. (Psalm 49:7–9)

No man except Yeshua ben Joseph, Jesus the son of Joseph, for Jesus is our Passover Lamb. He paid the ransom. Jesus said of himself, "For even the son of man came not to be served, but to serve, and to give his life as a ransom for many" (Mark 10:45).

This great promise of full redemption is well articulated in Paul's writing to the church in Corinth: "Therefore, if anyone is in Christ, he is a new creation; the old is gone, the new has come!" (2 Corinthians 5:17).

Perhaps the greatest fulfillment of Yom Kippur is not that Jesus died on the cross to redeem us but that he entered the most holy place to make atonement for us—that he, once and for all and for all the ages, with his own blood, entered a more perfect tabernacle, one not made by human hands, not of this creation, and there he cleansed our souls and our consciences from acts that lead to death. The Great Day of Atonement not only represents Jesus at Calvary but Jesus in the throne room of God, completing our full redemption.

> When Christ came as high priest of the good things that are already here, he went through the greater and more perfect tabernacle that is not man-made, that is to say, not a part of this creation. He did not enter by means of the blood of goats and calves; but he entered the Most Holy Place once for all by his own blood, having obtained eternal redemption. The blood of goats and bulls and the ashes of a heifer sprinkled on those who are ceremonially unclean sanctity them so that they are outwardly clean. How much more, then, will the blood of Christ, who through the eternal Sprit offed himself unblemished to God, cleanse our consciences from acts that lead to death, so that we may serve the living God! (Hebrews 9:11–14)

The Messiah's Seven Feasts

Feast	Jewish Purpose	Messianic Fulfillment
Passover (Pesach)	Celebrate salvation	Jesus is our Passover Lamb.
Unleavened Bread (Hag HaMotzi)	Personal purity before God	Jesus purifies us from sin.
Firstfruits (Reishit Katzir)	Celebration of new life	Jesus is first from the dead.
Weeks (Shavuot)	Fifty days to Sinai (law)	Fifty days to Pentecost and Holy Spirit
Trumpets (Yom Teru'ah)	Confession and mercy	Confession and grace
Day of Atonement (Yom Kippur)	Atonement (animal blood)	Atonement (blood of Christ)

The Seventh Feast: Tabernacles or Sukkot

From the Hebrew Text

The Feast of Tabernacles was the seventh and final feast and is the third feast observed in the month of Tishri. The Feast of Tabernacles began on the fifteenth day (Leviticus 23:33) and lasted for seven days. "Tabernacle" may not be the best translation for the word *sukkah* or its plural form, *sukkot*. Moses and the people had the tabernacle in the desert, the portable sanctuary. But *sukkot* is the Hebrew word for the temporary shelters they lived in during the forty years in the desert.[12] Like all the feasts, Tabernacles was layered in meaning. After the Feast of Trumpets with its ten days of repentance followed by the Great Day of Atonement; the people were freshly redeemed and atoned by the sacrifices. They were ready to celebrate. It was time to rejoice in renewed fellowship with Yahweh.

God wanted His people to honor Him and to acknowledge how He provided for their ancestors during their pilgrimage to Canaan. He gave them shelter, manna, and water. He was a loving shepherd for His flock. And when God used Joshua to lead the people into Canaan and subdued their enemies, the people received houses, farms, and lands—permanent places for people who must have been bone-tired and weary of the desert life and its temporary shelters. How amazing it must have been to take possession of lands and fields, to have houses they didn't build and wells they didn't dig. At long last, Abraham's people were home.

For the seven days of Tabernacles, the Jews built a small temporary shelter attached to their houses. The families stayed in these tabernacles for the weeklong feast. They worshiped each morning and evening, daily seasons of great worship and thanksgiving. The morning celebration revolved around water taken from the Pool of Siloam, to symbolize the water that kept their ancestors alive in the desert. The evening worship emphasized light and its symbolic meaning of God's guidance and illumination of truth. Giant candelabras, each with four large bowls filled with olive oil and giant wicks made from garments of the priests, blazed in the temple courts each night and symbolized the pillars of fire and cloud that guided the people in the desert. The Feast of Tabernacles, the final feast of the celebration calendar, was a heartfelt, worship-filled, and joyous celebration for all of Yahweh's blessings in bringing their forefathers to the Promise Land.

From the Greek Text

These great symbols of water and light are brought to a glorious fulfillment in Jesus, our Messiah, and to his teaching at the feast. David Brickner writes:

> The Gospels record that our Lord Jesus not only celebrated the festival, but He took traditional elements of the celebration and applied them to His own life and mission. We find this particularly in John 7 and 8 where Jesus uses two traditional symbols from the Feast of Tabernacles celebration, water and light, to help the people understand who He is and what He offers.[13]

Water to the Jews was life. No water in the desert meant no way to stay alive. Water ensured life for their crops, orchards, animals, and for themselves. Water became a dominant symbol of life and messianic fulfillment in the prophets. Light also was a powerful symbol of God. When God created light, he established a way to drive out the darkness, to sustain plant life, to guide His people in a pillar of fire. To celebrate festivals was to celebrate the light of the world.

The Messiah's Seven Feasts

Feast	Jewish purpose	Messianic fulfillment
Passover (Pesach)	Celebrate salvation	Jesus is our Passover Lamb.
Unleavened Bread (Hag HaMotzi)	Personal purity before God	Jesus purifies us from sin.
Firstfruits (Reishit Katzir)	Celebration of new life	Jesus is first from the dead.

Weeks (Shavuot)	Fifty days to Sinai (law)	Fifty days to Pentecost and Holy Spirit
Trumpets (Yom Teru'ah)	Confession and mercy	Confession and grace
Day of Atonement (Yom Kippur)	Atonement (animal blood)	Atonement (blood of Christ)
Tabernacles (Sukkot)	Yahweh in this life	The Son of God in heaven

All of the feasts were observed with wholehearted, full-throated praise. They were an integral part of the Yahweh covenant. The number of feasts is intentionally significant—*seven*, a perfect number reflecting a perfect God.

The feasts were also deeply messianic:

1. When death passed over the land of Egypt, it had its greatest fulfillment in Christ, our Passover Lamb.

2. The unleavened bread, eaten for a week, reminds us of Jesus forgiving sins and joining with us as we break bread with him in his memorial feast.

3. In Firstfruits, we joyfully give to God bringing Him an offering of thanksgiving, for the resurrection of His son, the first from among the dead!

4. Moses, fifty days after Ramses, received the law; so the Messiah, fifty days after ascending, sent the gift of the Holy Spirit to the world.

5. In the Feast of Trumpets, priests blew the shofars, alerting the worshipers to confession. With the trumpet call of God, Jesus will take us home forever.

6. In Yom Kippur, the Jews sought confession, repentance, and atonement with the high priest

sacrificing for all. In our Messiah, we have a great High Priest, offering a sacrifice once and for all—his life—to atone for our sins.

7. In Tabernacles, we see the temporary nature of this world, a world that is not our home, so we long for our heavenly home. In Jesus, our Messiah, God will bring us through the deserts of this life to that better place.

To better know the feasts is to better know Jesus. He fulfilled them. He lived and died in the shadow of these high, holy days of Israel. His own passion of the cross was experienced in the very heart of Passover, and his glorious resurrection took place in the week of Firstfruits. So how should we live? Shouldn't our days be filled with the glorious praise of his name, serving him with gladness, and a full heart of gratitude?

> In the past God spoke to our forefathers through the prophets at many times and in various ways, but in these last days he has spoken to us by his Son, whom he appointed heir of all things and through whom he made the universe. The Son is the radiance of God's glory and the exact representation of his being, sustaining all things by his powerful word. After he had provided purification for sins he sat down at the right hand of the Majesty in heaven. (Hebrews 1:1–3)

For Us Today

Some years ago, my wife's daily drive routed her through a busy downtown intersection. Each morning as she approached the intersection, she noticed a man standing on the corner, on the same corner, every day. In our city, it's fairly routine to see people standing on the corners, holding signs, and asking for money. However, this man wasn't holding a sign. He was holding a newspaper, selling them for a dollar. This went on for a few weeks. Then one day, she had a leading of the Spirit, and she engaged her heart regarding the man on the corner. So the next morning, and every morning thereafter, she lowered her window and handed him a dollar. He handed her a paper, a paper she didn't want. After a few weeks of the same routine, she began to feel the urge to reach out to him. She is like that. For her, this was a "God thing." In time, she learned that he was a disabled vet. She discovered that selling papers was his only employment. They became friendly within the context of a few moments at an intersection; after all, morning traffic maintains its urgent pace. They used each other's first name.

Then she dialed it up a notch. She started picking up some breakfast and coffee for him each morning. She was still giving him the dollar for a paper she didn't want. Each evening, she came home and shared her conversation with Roy (not his real name). She learned about his military experience and why he was disabled. She developed a relationship with him, twenty or thirty seconds at a time, Monday to Friday.

Then she dialed it up an even higher notch. One evening, she said, "Rick, I would like to invite Roy to have Thanksgiving with us." After regaining some composure, I replied with, "Why?" She said, "It's the right thing to do. He is poor and doesn't have any family or anywhere to go. We have plenty, and we need to invite him over." I dragged my feet for a while. We went back and forth for a few weeks, and then I gave in.

It's with some embarrassment that I admit my unhappiness with the idea. Invite a street-corner, paper-selling stranger into our home to share our Thanksgiving? This just didn't feel right. It will be awkward. What will we talk about? What will our children think? Is it safe for them? Our children were twenty-three and eighteen at the time. I conveyed these concerns to my wife, who just smiled and encouraged me to pray about it. And she asked if I would figure out how to get to his apartment.

I picked him up at eleven o'clock Thanksgiving morning. He was waiting for me on the curb, wearing brand-new jeans and a flannel shirt. It wasn't a comfortable neighborhood. It had lots of dilapidated buildings, barbed wire on the tops of walls, and litter on the streets. It was the kind of place you would never go to and didn't want to know about. It's where poor, disabled vets could afford to live.

We got to the house. I introduced him to our kids, and then we sat down to watch whatever football game was playing. He was quiet, polite, but seemed a bit awkward. Join the club. When the meal was ready, I turned off the game, gathered everyone to the table, said a blessing, and we enjoyed a splendid meal. He ate. He ate, and he ate, and he ate. Then he ate some more. And later, after dessert and seconds on dessert, I drove Roy home. But he didn't leave empty-handed. Danielle had packed up several bags of leftovers. For the first time in my Thanksgiving life, there would be no leftover turkey, no turkey gravy, or cranberry sauce, or stuffing, or mashed potatoes. There would be no pie, no cobbler with ice cream and fresh coffee. Yep, Roy got it all. He would come to more Thanksgivings. Danielle kept buying papers and breakfasts. We helped him with a monthly gift card to a local grocery store.

He got a phone and got into the habit of calling Danielle just about every day. Danielle shared her faith with him, talked to him about Jesus. She told him about God's love and purpose for his life. She encouraged him to find a church, which he did, and was blessed by its fellowship. Then one day, he just up and disappeared. Just like that. We tried to find him, but no luck. Roy was gone.

He taught me something about myself, a little self-discovery, the stuff you aren't ever proud of. Turns out there was a nasty little selfish streak in me. I didn't want to share my feast of Thanksgiving. I didn't want a stranger in my home, and I sure didn't want to give away all the leftovers!

Danielle's example was challenging and humbling. She taught me about compassion and the love of Christ and self-denial. Her example encouraged me to put the sermons I had preached into practice. Wow, Roy strikes again.

Isn't the real spirit of Thanksgiving about gratitude and sharing with others, even with strangers? Wasn't the idea of a national day of thanksgiving to gather with friends and family to pray and give thanks to God? How did I manage to make the feast of Thanksgiving something that was only about my convenience, relaxation, and comfort? I'm not really sure, but I did.

The seven feasts gave God's people the opportunity to remember Him and to recognize everything He had done and was doing for them. The feasts were about the nation's observance of thanksgiving, praise, and worship.

My holidays don't rival even one of the seven feasts. But sharing our family, our home, and our blessings with Roy deepened my appreciation for God and for His Son. I'm generally happy to acknowledge His blessings in my life. But it's in the very heart of Jesus that I see the true purpose of God—His salvation and atonement, His love for the world, and His giving the Holy Spirit to all who believe.

In the study of the seven feasts, I really learn about Jesus, our Messiah. The feasts help me see Jesus more completely.

They take me from the beginning to the end. Our Messiah was always there. Thank you, Danielle and Roy. And thank you, Jesus.

> But God demonstrates his own love for us in this:
> While we were still sinners Christ died for us.
>
> —Romans 5:8

5

Jonah, Immersed in Ministry

The book of Jonah has only four chapters, and they are really short chapters. Does this suggest that Jonah isn't much of a story? Is it too small to be very good? Don't worry. Few stories light up the imagination or fuel the fires of adventure like the story of Jonah. There's just something about a prophet on a boat who gets thrown into the sea and swallowed by a whale. I know. The great fish isn't identified. But if you are a child, especially if you are a third grade boy, and are listening to this story, then you just know that it was a giant whale that swallowed Jonah. The child can so easily imagine a giant whale rising from the deep, scooping him up, and gulping him down. And after three days in the great fish's belly? Well, three days later, the great fish puked him up, *puke* being the word a third grader would use.

Imagination fuels questions. Here are a few questions fueled by some imaginative boys:

- What was it like in the stomach of a whale?
- What did it smell like in there?
- Could Jonah sit up, stand up, or have to lie down?
- How did he breathe in there?
- Was it cold inside the fish?
- Did he eat seafood?

- Was it dark in there? Could he see?
- Where did he go to the bathroom?

There are so many questions and so many interesting thoughts to think about.

As third graders grow up, they discover other aspects to the story. They begin to ask, "What else does the Bible say about Jonah?" It turns out that in addition to the Old Testament book, the New Testament also mentioned him. Jesus referenced Jonah in some really interesting ways in answer to questions posed about his authority and miracles. This happened twice in Matthew and once in Luke. Although not named, I also believe that Jesus used Jonah's story in reference to his own resurrection in John 2:19.

To better understand Jesus and why he referenced Jonah, we need to answer a few questions. Here's one that comes to mind: Why would Jesus base an important part of his ministry on a prophet who frankly wasn't all that impressive? To find this and other answers, we need to go back to Jonah's story and take another look at the assignment he was given. Perhaps Jonah can point us forward to Jesus since Jesus, like Jonah, was also immersed in ministry.

From the Hebrew Text

Jonah was born about 800 BC and died approximately in 740 BC. He first appeared in scripture in 2 Kings 14:25. Outside the 2 Kings reference, he is known only in the OT from the book of Jonah. He grew up in Galilee, in the small village of Gath-hepher, a few miles north of Nazareth. It is interesting that he and Jesus were both raised in small villages located so close to each other. Not much is known about Jonah's background or personal life. He prophesied during the reign of Jeroboam II.

God's Call to Jonah

The story of Jonah is an amazing story. Although some debate its historical accuracy, or think it to be allegorical, I believe it really happened. Jonah was for real. He was a prophet called by God to go to Nineveh, the capital city of the Assyrian empire. The Lord wanted him to preach repentance to the Assyrians, but repentance with the promise of forgiveness. It's important to note the primary purpose of a prophet. Their purpose was to speak God's message to whomever and wherever He wanted His message spoken. The message was typically rooted in repentance. People were called to repentance, and through repentance, they could find forgiveness and blessing from God. If the people would turn away from their sin and turn their hearts toward God, then He would forgive. To paraphrase a typical prophetic message, "You are in rebellion against the Lord, your God, and He is angry, and his wrath burns against you. Repent of your evil ways and return wholeheartedly to the Lord, your God. If you fail to do so, then you will suffer for your hard-hearted, stiff-necked pride. But if you will humble yourself and turn to Him, then He will forgive your sins and restore blessings and prosperity to you."

Jonah Refused the Call

Preaching this message seemed to be more than Jonah was willing to do. He didn't want to go to Assyria, didn't want to preach to the Ninevites, and so he refused to go and, in fact, didn't go. It is perhaps understandable from a human perspective. For Jonah, Nineveh was an icon for evil; the Assyrians represented everything Jonah hated.[1] At that time in history, the Assyrians were making their presence known violently. They were causing great difficulty for Israel and had become a fierce enemy.

> It was then that Assyrian armies marched beyond their own borders to expand their empire, seeking booty to finance their plans for still more conquest and power. By the mid-ninth century BC, the Assyrian menace posed a direct threat to the small Syro-Palestine states to the west, including Israel and Judah.[2]

Jonah might have been more willing to go if it meant preaching wrath and judgment. He would have preferred for God to destroy the Assyrians (Jonah 4). But Jonah was unwilling to offer them the grace of God, or at least he was unwilling to risk the Assyrians repenting. Jonah knew that if Nineveh repented, then God, in His mercy, would forgive them. Forgiveness was something that Jonah didn't want the Assyrians to receive. As unlikely as it might have been for Nineveh to repent, Jonah wasn't about to take that chance.

Jonah refused to go to Nineveh. In an act of rebellion, he ran away from God, away from His calling. He went to Joppa, a port in southern Judah on the Mediterranean coast. He found a ship that was headed west and hopped aboard. Why go west? Was it because Nineveh was to the east, and Jonah wanted to get as far away as he possibly could? He found a ship set to sail in the opposite direction of where God had called him to go. Not good.

I wonder if some of the modern prophets among us would find Jonah's assignment a little tough to take? Can today's preachers harbor hatred, prejudice, and anger the same as anyone else? On the other hand, some of us might view the Nineveh calling as a great opportunity to advance our careers.

Jonah and the Great Fish

Jonah's boat cast off and sailed west into the Mediterranean Sea. It wasn't long before a huge storm created fear, stress, and conflict for the crew. It turned out they were a superstitious lot. They decided that Jonah was the problem, a bad omen, and the cause of the storm. The really sad part of this story is that Jonah, rather than resist them, actually encouraged them. It seemed he would prefer drowning in the ocean to preaching to the Assyrians (see Jonah 1:8–2). The crew was unsuccessful in getting the ship back to land, so they decided Jonah had to go. So up, over, and down he went into the churning, stormy sea. Normally that would be the end of the story, but God wasn't finished with Jonah. Maybe He wasn't finished with the Assyrians. So God caused a great fish to swallow Jonah, and swallowed he remained. He survived the great fish, no doubt by the providence of God. Three days later, Jonah was vomited up on the shore, not very far from Joppa, where he started.

Jonah Preaches to Nineveh

Jonah found himself even closer to the Assyrian capital. Once again, God called him to go and preach. This time, Jonah obeyed. He went to Nineveh and preached as he walked across the city, taking three days to do so. His message: repent or perish! And they did repent, the whole city! The king made sure that they did (Jonah 3:6–9).

Wouldn't that be considered a crowning moment in a prophet's career? Would it represent the high point of a prophetic ministry? An entire city of pagans turned to Yahweh! For most preachers, this would have been huge, like a lifetime achievement. They would have found a way to let everyone know. Tell the press, alert the media, and make sure that everyone everywhere knows every detail. Possible headlines might read:

"The Assyrians Get Saved!"
"Courageous Evangelist Reaches Thousands"
"Local Prophet Converts Hated Enemy"
"Soggy Preacher Preaches to Heathens"
"Fish-Stinking Evangelist Sees Sensational Success"

But that wasn't Jonah's reaction. He wasn't happy about all of them repenting. He didn't want them to repent. He wanted them to reject God and suffer the consequences. But God witnessed the Ninevites turn from evil, and He offered them His gracious compassion. God was slow to anger and abounded in love. He relented from sending calamity (Jonah 4:1–2).

Jonah was greatly displeased. He was angry with the Assyrians for turning to God and apparently wasn't all that happy with God either. In fact, he was so angry that he would just as soon die (Jonah 4:3). So Jonah climbed a hill and set up camp. He was waiting on the Lord. Waiting and hoping that perhaps God would change his mind, that maybe God's judgment of fire would still fall upon them? Jonah's message was plain and simple. On the first day, Jonah proclaimed, "Forty more days and Nineveh will be overturned."

Was he now up on the hillside, waiting for the forty days to end? Although he witnessed the whole city repent, was he still hopeful that Nineveh would burn?

But Nineveh didn't burn. The story concludes with God correcting Jonah for his lack of concern for the Assyrian people. Not much else is known about Jonah's life. There are stories and traditions suggesting he went home to Gath-hepher, lived out his life, and died peacefully. Until recently, there has been a tomb of Jonah in a small village close to Gath-hepher.[3] But how Jonah's life ended isn't what's really interesting; it's his contribution to the Messiah's teaching that matters most, as we will see.

Lessons from Jonah's Story

Jonah was a prophet immersed in ministry. He was immersed in the raging sea, then inside the great fish, and finally in the city of Nineveh. Jonah's story reminds us that God is the God of compassion. He stands ready to forgive, and He will forgive the most unforgivable person, people, city, or nation. As the Messiah taught in Matthew 7, so the story of Jonah teaches the value of getting the plank out of our eye. Before approaching the God of mercy, we should humble ourselves before the throne of grace. Jonah's story connects us to Jesus and his teaching. Jesus and Jonah— let's take a closer look.

From the Greek Text

The Pharisees Ask for a Sign

In his public ministry, Jesus was frequently challenged to provide a sign to validate his teaching. Those challenges were often posed as questions and came from his doubters and detractors. Here are two examples:

1. "Then some of the Pharisees and teachers of the law said to him, 'Teacher, we want to see a sign from you'" (Matthew 12:38).

2. "Then the Pharisees and Sadducees came to Jesus and tested him by asking him to show them a sign from heaven" (Matthew 16:1).

The Sign of Jonah

Twice in Matthew and once in Luke, Jesus used the story of Jonah in response to those who challenged his authority. In Luke, he used Jonah as a warning to the people of his generation. But why did Jesus refer to Jonah? Let's see if we can gain some insight.

> Then some of the Pharisees and teachers of the law said to him, "Teacher, we want to see a miraculous sign from you." He answered, "A wicked and adulterous generation asks for a miraculous sign! But none will be given it except the sign of the prophet Jonah. For as Jonah was three days and three nights in the belly of a huge fish, so the Son of Man will be three days and three nights in the heart of the earth. The men of Nineveh will stand up at the judgment with this generation and condemn it; for they repented at the preaching of Jonah, and now one greater than Jonah is here." (Matthew 12:38–41)

Those were strong words. Jesus was assertive and somewhat confrontational with these men. He was disturbed by their lack of faith and constant confrontations. They frequently demanded from him: "Give us a sign," "Show us a miracle," "Prove to us your authority to do these things." The stubborn, faithless responses of the Jews were in sharp contrast to the Assyrians' willingness to embrace Jonah's message. Jesus used Jonah, and the sign of Jonah, to lift up the people of Nineveh and their example of demonstrated faith. The pagan people of Nineveh actually believed and repented before God. This must have been difficult for the Jews to hear, to have Jesus elevate the Assyrians' faith above their own.

The Pharisees and Sadducees came to Jesus and tested him by asking him to show them a sign from heaven. He replied, "When evening comes, you say, 'It will be fair weather, for the sky is red,' and in the morning, 'Today it will be stormy, for the sky is red and overcast.' You know how to interpret the appearance of the sky, but you cannot interpret the signs of the times. A wicked and adulterous generation looks for a miraculous sign, but none will be given it except the sign of Jonah." Jesus then left them and went away. (Matthew 16:1–4)

Again, the sign of Jonah was the only sign Jesus offered. It's the only sign that will be offered to that wicked and adulterous generation. It's even stronger in Luke's account.

As the crowds increased, Jesus said, "This is a wicked generation. It asks for a miraculous sign, but none will be given it except the sign of Jonah. For as Jonah was a sign to the Ninevites, so also will the Son of Man will be to this generation. The Queen of the South will rise at the judgment with the men of this generation and condemn them; for she came from the ends of the earth to listen to Solomon's wisdom, and now one greater than Solomon is here. The men of Nineveh will stand up at the judgment with this generation and condemn it; for they repented at the preaching of Jonah, and now one greater than Jonah is here." (Luke 11:29–32)

Luke's account is the clearest in terms of what the sign of Jonah referred to. He recorded Jesus's words as, "For as Jonah was a sign to the Ninevites, so also will the Son of Man be to this generation." How was Jonah a sign to them?

How Was Jonah a Sign?

The question has to be asked. Why would the people of Nineveh listen to Jonah? What would cause them to stop and listen? Here are two ideas:

1. Was it the miraculous signs he performed?

    - Jonah's story revealed nothing about him performing miraculous signs.

    - He offered no divine proof or evidence to verify his authenticity.

    - He didn't perform even a single miraculous wonder to confirm his word.

2. Was it Jonah's prophetic personality?

    - Did he have a winning smile and a charming manner?

    - Was he able to capture them by his heartfelt words of concern?

    - Did he serve the people of Nineveh with many acts of kindness?

Jonah contains not a single miracle. God provided a great fish and an overnight gourd tree for shade, but those were His direct actions, not Jonah's. Nor was Jonah charming, compassionate, or caring. So again, if it wasn't his miracles or magnetism that won the Assyrians over, then what did?

Actually, I'm wondering why the Assyrians didn't attack and kill him on the spot. They weren't worshipers of Yahweh, the God of the Hebrews. Why would they care about Jonah's God and tolerate His prophet? This Jewish man walked into their city and spent three days preaching a message of destruction for Nineveh. They not only allowed him to preach, but they listened, believed, and repented. What happened?

Jonah: Bleached to Preach?

Was there something obvious that gave them pause and captured their attention?

Jonah was vomited onto the beach of the Mesopotamian coast, just west of the Assyrian Empire. Would there have been witnesses to this event? In fact, God may have made sure that there were plenty of witnesses when this happened. Can you imagine the great fish swimming up as close to the beach as he could and then opening his mouth and spewing the prophet up and out, right there on the sand? The manner in which Jonah entered Nineveh might have been what caused them to listen to him.

It's important to note that the Assyrians were a polytheistic people, and one of their gods was Dagon, the god of the sea and sea creatures. Dagon was known as the fish god.[4] He was depicted as part man and part fish. Henry Clay Trumbull makes this point:

> What better heralding, as a divinely sent messenger to Nineveh, could Jonah have had, than to be thrown up out of the mouth of a great fish, in the presence of witnesses, say on the coast of Phoenicia, where the fish-god was a favorite object of worship? Such an incident would have inevitably aroused the mercurial nature of Oriental observers, so that a multitude would be ready to follow the seemingly new avatar of the fish-god, proclaiming the story of his uprising from the sea, as he went on his mission to the city where the fish-god had its very center of worship.[5]

The Assyrians may have responded to Jonah because he appeared to have come right out of the ocean.

Another consideration would be Jonah's appearance. There are stories that tell of modern sailors being swallowed by whales. A story is told about a whaling ship named *Star of the East*. In 1896, *The New York Times*, as well as other newspapers, reported that a sailor fell into the ocean in the process of harpooning and capturing a whale. The whale swallowed him, but it was unknown to those on board, and the whale was brought on board the ship. Harvesting the blubber was a process that took a couple of days. Eventually the stomach was opened, and there was the sailor, curled up inside and still alive. The report is that his skin was bleached white by the whale's gastric juices.[6]

After three days in a sea creature's stomach, the acids would have bleached Jonah's skin and, by the process of digestion, removed all his body hair. When Jonah was hurled out of the sea creature, witnesses would have been stunned and assumed that he was a specially sent messenger of the sea gods. Jonah's entry into Nineveh may have provided instant credibility as a divine messenger of Dagon, perhaps even more so than if he had obeyed God to begin with and obediently went to Nineveh when he was told to do so.[7] The Lord, our God, carries out his purpose one way or another. He always has.

Was a bleached-white Jonah, smelling of dead fish, without hair or a beard, and with a large crowd of witnesses, the sign that made the Assyrians pay attention to him? Was this their "sign of Jonah"? Jonah didn't perform miraculous signs. He *was* the sign. At first, the Assyrians may have given credit to Dagon for this divine messenger from the sea. We will never know. Whatever the reasons for the Assyrians listening to him, whether divine or natural, they did, in fact, listen. They didn't arrest, attack, or kill him. As amazing as it may seem, they believed and repented.

Jonah's preaching came with true authority, the authority and power that is the Word of God. They may have started with Dagon, but they ended with Yahweh. Once they accepted Jonah as a sign from his God, then they accepted him, believed his preaching, and turned to the one true God of heaven and earth.

For Us Today

We are born with a spirit of autonomy. We like living with the sense that we are empowered. I love being sovereign over my life; it's just that I tend to be really bad at it. Jesus taught something different. He spoke of self-denial versus self-empowerment. He advocated lowering ourselves instead of exalting ourselves. Our Messiah valued mercy over judgment, love over hate, and humility over arrogance. He taught the forgiveness of others even if they don't apologize first, or ever. His earliest recorded teachings began with these values. His kingdom is built on them; his is a kingdom of conscience.

Jonah reminds us that God loves everyone, that He alone is the righteous judge, and at no time has He ever transferred that responsibility to me. Jonah didn't follow his call to the Assyrians; it wasn't a mission he wanted. He was a prophet to God's people, and Nineveh wasn't God's people. Maybe he thought that if God destroyed Nineveh, it would alter Israel's future for the better. But that wasn't Jonah's call to make, was it? Jonah reminds us that God is calling us to serve. What has the Messiah called you to do? What is your calling? Are you a believer immersed in ministry? Here is a story for you.

I was standing in line, waiting to board my flight. I had been invited to spend some time with a church that was working through some issues. I was asked to consult, teach, and help in any way I could, and it was important work. I hoped to leave them encouraged, strengthened, and better prepared to serve. I had been called.

While waiting to board my flight, a young man who was oddly dressed came up to ask if this was the flight to Chicago. I told him it was, and he said, "Cool." It was his first time to fly, and he wasn't sure about his boarding pass or where to sit or what line to stand in. He was a young guy, maybe eighteen or nineteen. He was wearing jeans that were way too big and worn way too low. He was wearing a sweatshirt with a hood, which was up. It wasn't cold. The airline had open seating, which contributed to his confusion. I was near the front of the first group to board; he was near the back of the last group to board. I quickly got the aisle seat I wanted and sat there, hoping for a half-full flight. After most of the passengers had boarded, there was still an open seat next to me, and I was thinking I might have a flight without a seatmate. But just as the last passengers were getting on, I looked up and made eye contact with the hoody. He recognized me, smiled, and asked, "Can I sit there?" I said, "Sure" and silently sighed. He seemed pleased to have found someone he knew to sit with.

He quickly began chatting about things. I wasn't rude, but I did want to focus on the material that I would be presenting. He finally got the message, and so he engaged the person sitting by the window. And he did so for the remainder of the flight. As the plane was landing and I was thinking about my connecting flight, he turned to me and said, "I think it's really cool that you are into God." I was speechless. He then said, "I'm a Christian too. Hey, you want to see my Bible?" He reached into this old ratty-looking bag he had under the seat in front of him and pulled out a paperback Bible that was dog-eared, worn out, and falling apart. He showed me some of his favorite scriptures. As the plane docked at the gate, he said that he saw my Bible and notes on the tray table. Then he asked if I was a pastor. "Yes, I am," I said. At that moment, the bell sounded, everyone unbuckled, the aisle people jumped up, and well, you know the rest.

"I think it's really cool that you are in to God."

In that moment, I felt like God probably wasn't very pleased with me, and that Jesus wouldn't have approved of me, like I had grieved the Holy Spirit. I had sized up the young man, decided he was odd, and concluded he wasn't someone to pay attention to and dismissed him.

It's not that I thought of him as a Ninevite. He wasn't my enemy. I didn't hate him. It was more about not wanting to think about him at all. I had important work to do, and in that moment, he just wasn't important.

"I think it's really cool that you are in to God."

Jesus was the master at seeing people, of making connections, at finding lost sheep. He wore his compassion on his shirtsleeve. "For even the Son of Man came not to be served, but to serve, and give his life as a ransom for many." I'm one of those he came to serve, one of those he came to seek. I was lost, and he found me.

Jonah reminds us that being immersed in ministry is a good thing. He also reminds us that ministry is often a mission to people and places not of our choosing. Sometimes we sail west when God has called us east. It isn't Messiah-like. In Israel, there was one greater than Jonah performing miracles, wonders, and signs. He was healing, helping, and serving the least of his brothers. Still there were many who rejected him. He would give them one final sign of his true identity and divine authority. Think of it as "the sign of all signs." It was, of course, the empty tomb.

So take a moment to reflect. Are you rooted in the center of His will? Though none of us are perfect, or asked to be, we are still called to lift up our Messiah, embrace him, and embrace his purpose for our lives. Is there someone odd trying to sit next to you? Yes, it's a metaphor for those we might otherwise ignore, neglect, or dismiss.

6

The Branches

Growing up, I had a strict standard for assessing the value of a tree. A really good tree was very tall with very low branches. In my world, trees existed to be climbed and therefore needed to have branches low enough to pull myself up. After that, it was only a matter of courage as to how high I could climb. I loved trees.

Interesting trees of all shapes and sizes exist all over the world. Until my first trip to the Holy Land, I had little awareness of the trees in scripture such as figs, cedars, pomegranates, date palms, and especially olive trees. Having traveled throughout Israel, not only did I sees orchards and groves of many kinds but also was able to engage with their biblical value. Learning more about the Bible's trees has led to greater insight to Jesus's teaching, especially his parables. The greater insights have also come from the presence of trees in the writings of the prophets. Although all of the trees, vines, and bushes in scripture have meaning and purpose, for me, there are none more significant than the olive tree.

Visiting the garden of Gethsemane was a deeply moving experience. It was like being on sacred ground, for it's the place where Jesus prayed and where his sweat fell like drops of blood. It's the place his drowsy disciples slept and where Judas betrayed him. It's just so very enriching to be in such a beautiful place, with the amazing view of Jerusalem and the Temple Mount across the Kidron Valley.

The garden of Gethsemane is an olive orchard. The trees were beautiful and surprisingly interesting. Some were ancient, as many as 1800 years old. With olive trees, the older they get, the more gnarled, twisted, and cracked their trunks become. Some of them had trunks that were split open and appeared to be hollow inside, and I wondered how they kept from collapsing under the weight of the limbs. However, no matter how ancient the tree, their leaves, branches, and fruit looked young and vibrant.

The Olive Tree in Scripture

In Israel, olive trees[1] can be found scattered about the countryside, a few at a time or in small groves. In scripture, groves and orchards are referred to as gardens, as in the garden of Gethsemane. They aren't "gardens" as we would use the word but groves planted for commercial purposes, primarily for the olive oil.

In first-century Palestine, the amount of olive trees a village had could determine its level of prosperity. A family with mature olive trees was more prosperous than a family without them. Building prosperity with olive trees was a long-term process due to their slow growth rate.[2] Therefore, mature olive trees were highly prized.

Here are a few examples of the importance of the olive tree and its oil:

1. The olive tree is referred to as the king of trees (Judges 9:8–9).

2. Anointing the temple, priests, kings, and prophets was done with olive oil.

3. The lamps and the menorah were fueled by olive oil, with olives grown in Israel and brought and presented to the temple as a tithe from the growers.

4. David, in Psalms 52:8, referred to himself as a flourishing olive tree.

The olive tree has great significance in scripture. For instance, it was used as a metaphor of Yahweh's relationship with Israel. Perhaps within the scriptures, the olive tree's use and symbolism was used most dramatically in the prophets. They used the olive tree, the olives, and their oil as symbols for Judah, Israel, and for many messianic references. We will examine "olive tree" texts in Jeremiah, Ezekiel, and Zechariah. First, let's take a look at why the prophets were necessary, why God called them to preach.

The Historical Background of Israel's Fall

The nation of Israel failed, becoming the divided kingdom. After they became separate nations, they continued to deteriorate. Ultimately they were defeated by their enemies and taken captive into exile. But how did all of that happen?

What Happened to Israel?

Israel was once a thriving kingdom under Yahweh's leadership and guidance. But in time, the people asked for a king to rule over them, like all the nations around them. For 120 years, Kings Saul, David, and Solomon led Israel. They were not perfect men. They made mistakes, and they sinned. But of the three kings, Solomon especially dropped the ball. It's all the more egregious that Solomon ended up the way he did since God had granted him great wisdom. Toward the end of his life, he didn't apply his wisdom, and it proved horribly costly.

Richard N. Fyffe

Solomon and His Foreign Wives

God had clearly commanded the people not to take wives from among the pagans. He was abundantly clear.

> Be careful not to make a treaty with those who live in the land; for when they prostitute themselves to their gods and sacrifice to them, they will invite you and you will eat their sacrifices. And when you choose some of their daughters as wives for your sons and those daughters prostitute themselves to their gods, they will lead your sons to do the same. Do not make any idols. (Exodus 34:15–16)

> Do not intermarry with them. Do not give your daughters to their sons or take their daughters for your sons, for they will turn your sons away from following me to serve other gods, and the Lord's anger will burn against you and will quickly destroy you. (Deuteronomy 7:3–4)

Solomon chose to ignore the will of God regarding foreign wives. Toward the end of his reign, his compromises caused Israel to fall headlong into idolatry. He disregarded God's commandments by making treaties with pagan governments and by taking wives from among their people. His disregard for God led him into massive polygamy and enabled his pagan wives to practice their idolatry.

> He had seven hundred wives of royal birth and three hundred concubines and his wives led him astray. As Solomon grew old his wives turned his heart after other gods, and his heart was not fully devoted to The Lord his God, as the heart of his father David had been. (1 Kings 11:3–5)

> On a hill east of Jerusalem, Solomon built a high place for Chemosh the detestable god of Moab, and for

Molek the detestable god of the Ammonites. He did the same for all his foreign wives, who burned incense and offered sacrifices to their gods. (1 Kings 11:7–8)

For this is what the Lord, the God of Israel says, "See, I am going to tear the kingdom out of Solomon's hand." (1 Kings 11:31)

The nation became two countries, Judah and Israel, but they largely continued in idolatry, led by mostly weak and wicked kings.

So God raised up prophets to warn the kings. Their message was simple: "Repent, for the wrath of God is at hand. But if you won't repent, God will raise up your enemies to carry you into captivity. But a remnant will be spared. One day, the Anointed of God, the Son of David, will come and will call the houses of Judah and Israel to Mount Zion and to the Messiah's kingdom."

The prophets came, and they prophesied. Their messages contained language the people would understand and also often contained illustrations from their culture to make the prophecies clearer and poignant. The olive tree became a strong symbol for the prophets, as will be seen from Ezekiel, Jeremiah, and Zachariah. The people of God were His olive tree, which he planted and loved.

Israel As an Olive Tree

The Lord called you a thriving olive tree with fruit beautiful in form. But with the roar of a mighty storm he will set it on fire, and its branches will be broken. The Lord Almighty, who planted you, has decreed disaster for you, because the house of Israel and the house of Judah have done evil and provoked

> me to anger by burning incense to Baal. (Jeremiah 11:16–17)

What happened to that thriving, beautiful olive tree? As the nation plunged into further idolatry, Israel's sins were too immense to let stand. The beautiful tree would not continue. The nation was ripped apart; the beautiful olive tree was ripped and burned.

> He asked me, "What do you see?" I answered, "I see a solid gold lamp stand with a bowl at the top and seven lights on it, with seven channels to the lights. Also there are two olive trees by it, one on the right of the bowl, and the other on its left." (Zechariah 4:2–3)

The kingdom was torn in two and then taken into exile. But the Messiah's day was coming, and prophets gave hope to the people. Zechariah's prophecy offered much hope of a unified Israel, with the nations flowing to Zion through the power of the Holy Spirit. Let's now take a closer look as Zechariah.

Who Were Zechariah and Zerubbabel?

Zechariah was a sixth-century prophet, probably of priestly descent.[3] His prophetic ministry took place in Jerusalem and Judah about 520 BC. His ministry included assisting Zerubbabel in the completion of the second temple. Zerubbabel was a grandson of Jehoiachin, a former king of Judah who was exiled into captivity in 586 BC. About 536 BC, Cyrus, king of Persia, sent Zerubbabel and roughly fifty thousand Jews back to Jerusalem. He served as governor of Judea and began rebuilding the temple.

The Symbols of Zechariah's Vision

So far, we have noted the symbolism of the olive tree, reviewed Israel's fall and historical background, and understood that they were once a thriving and beautiful olive tree. Now let's briefly review the symbols of Zechariah's vision.

> Then I asked the angel, "What are these two olive trees on the right and the left of the lamp-stand?" Again I asked him, "What are these two olive branches beside the two gold pipes that pour out the golden oil?" He replied, "Do you not know what these are?" "No, my Lord," I said. So he said, "These are the two who are anointed to serve The Lord of all the earth." (Zechariah 4:11–4)

Each of the symbols in his vision contained significant meaning. The vision included the following elements with symbolic relevance.

1. The two olive trees: fallen Judah and Israel, scattered among the nations

2. The two branches: the two anointed to serve the Lord

3. The golden oil: the word of God and the Holy Spirit

4. The two gold pipes: the prophets or servants carrying God's word

5. The gold lampstand, the temple's menorah: the light of God

6. The bowl: the Holy Spirit

7. The seven channels: the Spirit's power to fuel the lamps

8. The seven lamps: God's eyes, looking, searching for His people

Who Are the Two Branches Anointed to Serve?

Notice that each tree had a single branch that held a golden pipe that carried the golden oil to the bowl. I believe the two branches, one from each tree, were symbols for Moses and Elijah.

Moses was from the tribe of Levi, the priesthood. He was the deliverer of Israel from Egypt, wielded the staff of God, and stood on holy ground. He received the law on Sinai and led Israel across the desert, providing the lifesaving water. He was Yahweh's choice to lead the people to Canaan, to fulfill His land promises to Abraham.

Elijah was from Tishbe in Gilead, east of the Jordan River (1 Kings 17:1). He was from the tribe of Gad and was the prophet who stood up against King Ahab and his wicked queen, Jezebel. Elijah stood on Mount Carmel and challenged the 850 prophets and prophetesses to determine who was truly God: Yahweh or Baal. Elijah emerged the winner in an overwhelming victory (1 Kings 18). The great prophet Elijah didn't taste death but instead was taken up to heaven in a whirlwind (2 Kings 2:1,11).

Moses and Elijah, two great leaders. One represented the south and the other the north of the two kingdoms. Moses was the lawgiver and deliverer, and Elijah was the great prophet who stood against an idolatrous king in Ephraim. They were two great leaders who became symbols for wholehearted devotion to God.

Consider these thoughts about Moses and Elijah:

- Both were deliverers: Moses to Canaan, and Elijah to Yahweh.

- Both were infused with the Spirit of God.

- Both were on the Mount of Transfiguration with Jesus, the manifestations of the law, the prophets, and the Messiah.

Zechariah's vision pictured Judah and Israel as olive trees, with each tree having an anointed servant to serve the Lord of all the earth, not by their strength but by the power of God's Spirit. The golden pipes carried the sacred oil, for the trees themselves were messianic. The Holy Spirit, the expression of God's power, would flow through the golden pipes into the bowl to ignite and fuel the lamps of God. His eyes would search the earth to bring His people to Mount Zion and the Son of David. There would be one people, called by one name, living to bring glory and honor to the Lord God. Now let's consider other prophets in light of Zechariah's olive-tree vision of unity and messianic blessings.

Israel and Judah Reunification

> This is what The Lord Almighty, the God of Israel, says: "When I bring them back from captivity, the people in the land of Judah and its towns will once again use these words: The Lord bless you, O righteous dwelling, O sacred mountain." (Jeremiah 31:23)

> The word of the Lord came to me: "Son of man, take a stick of wood and write on it, 'Belonging to Judah and the Israelites associated with him.' Then take another stick of wood, and write on it, 'Ephraim's stick, belonging to Joseph and all the house of Israel associated with him.' Join them together into one stick so that they will become one in your hand... Hold before their eyes the sticks you have written

> on and say to them, 'This is what the Sovereign Lord says: I will take the Israelites out of the nations where they have gone, I will gather them from all around and bring them back into their own land. I will make them one nation in the land, on the mountains of Israel. There will be one king over all of them and they will never again be two nations or be divided into two kingdoms.'" (Ezekiel 37:15–17, 20–22)

The Hebrew word used for *stick* is *ates*, meaning "tree." It's translated as "a tree, plank, stick, or timber." The same word *ates* is used in Genesis for "fruit-bearing trees" and for "every tree" from which Adam and Eve could eat. It's the same word used for "tree of life" and for "the tree of the knowledge of good and evil."

Yahweh wasn't telling Ezekiel to "hold a tree in each hand." But it's likely that the sticks or branches Ezekiel held in his hand were broken off a tree, probably an olive tree. Refer back to Jeremiah's prophecy and how the branches were to be broken off the olive tree.

God instructed Ezekiel to write "belonging to Judah and the Israelites belonging to them" and then "belonging to Ephraim and Israelites belonging to them." Who were the Israelites that belonged to Judah and to Ephraim?

1. Southern kingdom: Judah and Benjamin, and the Levites.

2. Northern kingdom: the remaining ten tribes, also known as Ephraim.

Who was "Ephraim"? Israel's first king, Jeroboam, was from Ephraim, as was his capital, the city of Samaria. Here are two references:

The Lord will bring on you and on your people and on the house of your father a time unlike any since Ephraim broke away from Judah. (Isaiah 7:17)

I know all about Ephraim; Israel is not hidden from me. Ephraim, you have now turned to prostitution; Israel is corrupt. (Hosea 5:3)

Israel and Judah Unite Under the King

Ezekiel's prophecy pointed to a time when the house of Jeroboam-Ephraim would make peace with the house of David-Judah.

My servant David will be king over them, and they will all have one shepherd. I will make a convent of peace with them; it will be an everlasting covenant. I will establish them and increase their numbers and I will put my sanctuary among them forever. My dwelling place will be with them; I will be their God, and they will be my people. Then the nations will know that I the Lord make Israel holy, when my sanctuary is among them forever. (Ezekiel 37:24, 26–28)

This picture of spiritual reunification could only be accomplished through the Son of David, the Wonderful Counselor and Prince of Peace, who would be King and Shepherd over the people. These virtues would be necessary for bringing the people out of hatred and conflict and restoring them to unity, harmony, and peace.

And he will be called Wonderful Counselor, Mighty God, Everlasting Father, Prince of Peace. (Isaiah 9:6)

In that day the Root of Jesse will stand as a banner for the peoples; the nations will rally to him, and his place of rest will be glorious. Ephraim's jealousy will vanish, and Judah's enemies will be cut off; Ephraim will not

be jealous of Judah nor Judah hostile toward Ephraim.
(Isaiah 11:10, 13)

In Summary of the Hebrew Prophecies

These prophetic pictures portray two kingdoms divided by history, rebellion, and exile coming together under the Messiah. This was Zechariah's vision, as it was Isaiah's, Jeremiah's, and Ezekiel's.

From the Greek Text

All believers worldwide, in all time zones and in all the ages, exist in the Messiah's glorious kingdom. Zechariah's vision encompasses Jews and Gentiles alike, for we are bound together under the Messiah's banner of peace. The menorah's seven lights are the eyes of God, searching and seeking to save those who are lost. But how did the Gentiles get in? How were the nations allowed to come to Mount Zion?

The Olive Tree and the Gentiles

Paul gave a dynamic metaphor of unity and fellowship in the Messiah's kingdom.

> If some of the branches have been broken off, and you, though a wild olive shoot, have been grafted in among the others and now share in the nourishing sap from the olive root, do not boast over those branches. If you do, consider this: You do not support the root, but the root supports you. You will say then, "Branches were broken off so that I could be grafted in." Granted. But they were broken off because of their unbelief, and you stand by faith. Do not be arrogant, but be afraid. For if God did not spare the natural branches, he will not spare you either. (Romans 11:17–21)

Paul utilized the OT language and picture of the olive tree. He taught that the messianic olive tree, with Abrahamic roots, supports the branches. The branches exist by faith, not by birthright. The unbelieving branches were pruned off, creating room for Gentile branches to be grafted in. It's a picture of grace, mercy, and hope. Paul offers similar language of unity and hope to the Ephesians.

The Unity of Jews and Gentiles

> Therefore, remember that formerly you who are Gentiles by birth and called "uncircumcised" by those who call themselves "the circumcision," remember that at that time you were separate from Christ, excluded from citizenship in Israel and foreigners to the covenants of the promise, without hope and without God in the world. But now in Christ Jesus you who once were far away have been brought near through the blood of Christ. For he himself is our peace. (Ephesians 2:11–14)

Peter's Promise of the Holy Spirit

Peter and the apostles probably preached from the southern steps of the Temple Mount. Peter's message offered forgiveness of sins and the gift of the Holy Spirit. His message of the resurrected Nazarene brought the crowd to a sacred moment: they asked what they must do to be saved. His message focused to a fine point of faith in action.

> Peter replied, "Repent and be baptized, every one of you, in the name of Jesus Christ so that your sins may be forgiven. And you will receive the gift of the Holy Spirit. The promise is for you and your children and for all who are far off, for all whom the Lord our God will call." (Acts 2:38–39)

God has been calling those who are far off ever since His son ascended and poured out the Spirit on all mankind. Zechariah's vision included the day of Jew and Gentile salvation. His prophecy concluded picturing the nations of the earth flowing to Mount Zion to worship the King! Those who came were welcomed to participate in the most joyful of all the feasts, the Feast of Tabernacles.[4]

Paul wrote this marvelous statement:

> You are all sons of God through faith in Christ Jesus, for all of you who were baptized into Christ have been clothed with Christ. There is neither Jew nor Greek, slave nor free, male nor female, for you are all one in Christ Jesus. If you belong to Christ, then you are Abraham's seed, and heirs according to the promise. (Galatians 3:26–29)

There is one glorious olive tree with remnant branches and branches of believing Gentiles, for by faith we are all children of Abraham. One glorious tree with roots so deep and strong it supports the branches of all the peoples of the earth—each one nourished by the radiance of God's Spirit.

The eyes of God continue to look, for the Redeemer of mankind came to seek and to save the lost: Jews and Gentiles, all races, cultures, and all people everywhere. It's a kingdom with room for everyone, for those just like Abram, Moses, Jonah, and the Ninevites.

By embracing Zechariah's vision of the two olive trees, we are pushed forward to embrace and connect with Jesus, our Messiah. It all points to him![5]

> I did not see a temple in the city, because the Lord God Almighty and the Lamb are its temple. The city does not need the sun or the moon to shine on it, for the glory of God gives it light and the Lamb is

its lamp. The nations will walk by its light and the kings of the earth will bring their splendor into it. (Revelation 21:22–24)

For Us Today

In grade school, my two best friends were Bobby and Mitch (not their real names). We played after school and were together as much as we could on Saturdays and were inseparable in summer. We did whatever there was to do, and when we had nothing to do, we invented something.

Our neighborhood had alleys. The alleys were an amazing place to play if you were eight years old. There was always lots of cool stuff set out for trash pickup. The alleys were dirty, messy, and a bit unsafe. I was instructed to stay out of the alleys. "Don't play in the alleys, Ricky" was the message. So, of course, I played in them whenever I could.

That summer, we discovered flipping matches. Flipping matches was tearing a match from a matchbook, striking it against the emery board with your index finger, and then flipping it or launching it toward someone, like one of your friends. My friend's parents smoked, and getting matchbooks was easy. This was so great. It was stupid and foolish, but it was so great.

On one hot afternoon, we were enjoying our new game. We were in the alley, acting cool, trying to singe the hair off each other and laughing our heads off. Now, fifty years ago, the awareness of certain things had not yet come of age—specifically when the men on our block changed their oil, they drained it into a container and then put the container in the alley for trash collection. Often the oil spilled or got knocked over. It was common for the ground where the garbage cans stood to be soaked with used motor oil. Do you see where this is headed?

There we were, young and foolish, flipping matches next to our wooden fence, by our garbage cans. Sure enough, before we could say *uh-oh*, the ground was on fire, and so was the fence. The three of us looked at each other, panicked, and ran like scalded dogs. They ran out of the alley and straight home, leaving me with my panic, my fear and my back fence on fire. I ran around to our front door, yelling that our fence was on fire. My two older brothers looked out back, ran out, and got the water hose working. We had a pool, and one of them grabbed a bucket and started scooping water and throwing it on the fence. The fence didn't burn down, but there was a whole section that was extra crispy. And then Dad came home. My grandma and brothers had already informed my mom, who wasn't there at the time, about the fire. She was waiting for him. I was quickly brought front and center. I lied, I cried, and I blamed it on someone else. Dad questioned me nearly forever. Finally, acting on some kind of hunch or parental instinct, he said, "Okay, Rick, I believe you, but do me a favor and empty your pockets." I said, "Yes, sir." And when I did, out came the matchbook. "Where did you get the matches, Rick?" Dad asked. My parents didn't smoke; neither did we keep matchbooks in the house. Caught and busted, I blamed my friends. But it was over, and I was guilty. I was a liar and a firebug.

I did a number of things wrong that day:

1. I was in a place I shouldn't have been.

2. I was playing with fire and had been taught not to.

3. I started a fire I didn't want to start—but, wow, there are consequences!

My tears didn't save me. My fears didn't spare me. But there was a single and positive element to that no-good, terrible, horrible day—it was my mom.

While Dad was angry, she was calm and a peacemaker. I was guilty, and she knew it, and I would face the consequences. She sat with me, soothed my fears, dried my tears, and made me feel better. She reminded me about some good things that were coming up. There were camping trips planned, some fun family events, and some other cool things. And from her words, I slowly realized that I was going to be okay. It wasn't the end. My mom was a shining beacon with her vision of a brighter future, a vision that still included me. Thanks, Mom.

Like Solomon before me, I knew I was doing wrong, but I did it anyway. When you play with fire, it's likely that someone, or something, is going to get burned. It happened to me, and it happened to Solomon. It burned him, his family, and his kingdom. He lost everything, and it plunged the nation into darkness. But like my mom, the prophet Zechariah had a vision of a brighter future. He pointed to better times when the Messiah would gather them and restore them back to the Father. He would make the peace.

Jesus, the Prince of Peace and the Shepherd of our souls! Thank you, Messiah.

Part II

How Jesus Fulfilled Our Messianic Needs

7

Sheep, Shepherds, and Goats

Our family's roots grew mostly in urban soil. We weren't raised in rural America with its fields of green and golden wheat but in large cities with their tall buildings and crowded freeways. The agrarian countryside's farms, flocks, and herds were beyond our experience. When I was little, our family visited a petting zoo, which, among other animals, had some sheep and goats. The goats had big horns, which scared me, and it just seemed that the big-horned goats didn't like me very much. So mostly I petted the sheep and the lambs, which were small, soft, and nonthreatening. This was as close as I came to experiencing a flock culture. But I have visited countries with flock cultures.

Israel is such a fascinating country to visit. It has a rich heritage and is, of course, the land of our Messiah. It's not a large country, just barely bigger than New Jersey. Their Ministry of Foreign Affairs states the country is 85 miles wide and 290 miles long. Although small, Israel does have an especially interesting environment, offering two distinct climates. Galilee to the north is green and fertile due to its rich soil and abundant water. To the south are Israel's deserts and, with noted exceptions, void of vegetation. The southern wilderness rises up with majestic mountains and has a beauty all its own. Each region is unique, incredibly interesting, and together served as the homeland for God's people.

Richard N. Fyffe

Although Israel has modern, metropolitan cities, it nevertheless has retained its culture of sheep and goats. I would have thought that the breadbasket region in the north would be the natural location for raising flocks and herds, but it's not, at least it wasn't in Jesus's day. Back then, most of the flocks and herds were raised in the south, in the open desert lands and hills of ancient Samaria and Judea.[1] Does the idea of raising flocks in the desert seem counterintuitive? Why would shepherds choose the harsher environment? It had little to no water. The arid climate didn't encourage much grass for grazing. There was a constant threat of danger from jackals and other predators, some of them human. Yet the desert was where most of the sheep and goats were raised.[2]

Did Israel being the "land of milk and honey" explain the desert flock culture? One perspective suggests that Galilee was the land of honey, referring to the honeybees and the crops, orchards, and vineyards. If Galilee was the land of honey, then Judea's desert was the land of milk, perhaps referring to goat's milk. The desert offered wide-open spaces and plenty of room for the herds and flocks. Typically, the farmers of Galilee wouldn't want the sheep grazing in their fields since they would graze on the plants down to the roots. The land of milk and honey was a place where sheep, goats and shepherds could coexist with orchards, vineyards, and farmers—not on the same land but in their respective regions in the north and south. Both were necessary for the success of Israel's agrarian culture, and both existed as the promised inheritance to Abraham's descendants.

The Bible contains significant references to sheep, shepherds, and goats, allowing us to observe the unique nature of the shepherd-flock relationship. The connection between the shepherd and his flock was very strong. He was intertwined with his flock.[3] Scripture also provides some meaningful insights to Jesus, of how he functioned and served as a shepherd, especially with the lost sheep of Israel. By learning more about the desert flocks and their shepherds, we see more fully how committed Jesus is to shepherding each of us. Let's first explore the idea of shepherds from the Old Testament.

From the Hebrew Text

God As a Shepherd

Scripture has many names for God, as well as many metaphors, symbols, and word pictures. We are familiar with *Father, Fortress, Savior, Rock, Judge,* and with *Adonai* and YAHWEH. But arguably, one of the strongest and most frequent pictures of God is that of the Shepherd.[4] God was the true Shepherd of Israel and revealed His love and affection for His people through the shepherd-flock relationship. Here are some examples of God as the Shepherd:

- "The God who has been my shepherd all my life" (Genesis 48:15)

- "Because of the Shepherd, the rock of Israel" (Genesis 49:24).

- "The Lord is my Shepherd" (Psalms 23:1).

- "Be their shepherd and carry them forever" (Psalms 28:9).

- "He tends his flock like a shepherd: He gathers the lambs in his arms, and carries them close to his heart; he gently leads those that have young" (Isaiah 40:11).

- "I have not run away from being your shepherd" (Jeremiah 17:16).

- "God will save them...the flock of His people" (Zechariah 9:16).

Since Israel was steeped in the herd/flock culture, the people could easily relate to Yahweh as their Shepherd; they knew exactly what that meant.

God's Shepherds

Throughout Old Testament history, God looked to Israel's leaders to shepherd His people. Some of the best-known personalities in the Bible were shepherds. Here are some of the more famous shepherds:

- Abel
- Abraham
- Lot
- Isaac
- Jacob
- Rachel
- Moses
- David
- Jeremiah
- Amos

From Abel to Amos, shepherds were present in the Old Testament. The work of shepherding required a full commitment. The shepherd cared for his animals, knowing and calling each one by name, and was a constant presence. If a sheep wandered off and got lost, he would search for it to bring it back to the flock. If the animal were weak, sick, or injured, he would hold it in his arms or carry it across his shoulders. A shepherd maintained a clear eye, always watching for potential danger, for he was the flock's only protection. The spiritual applications to being a shepherd of souls are staggering. Ultimately, I'm not sure which would be more challenging to shepherd: sheep or people. But the Lord called those He wanted to care for the flock of Israel.

Moses was a shepherd in Midian for forty years and then became the shepherd of the Hebrew people, leading them across the deserts. There were moments when he was not the spiritual leader they needed. Israel's kings and priests also had their struggles in shepherding the nation. In the days of our Messiah, the Pharisees, rabbis, and elders of the people were guilty of neglecting the flock and leaving them at risk. Having as many weaknesses as strengths, Israel's shepherds demonstrated that no man or group of men could shepherd His flock as effectively as their Lord.

Ultimately, all of us would need a better shepherd. But before we get to the Good Shepherd, let's take a closer look at some of Israel's keepers of the flock.

David As a Shepherd-King of Israel

Israel looked out and saw that kings ruled the nations around them. So they asked to have a king to reign over them too. Although Samuel warned them in great detail about the hardships and destructive consequences of their request, they nevertheless still wanted a king, and so God gave them kings. Within their monarchial culture, the king was still thought of as Israel's shepherd. David, Israel's second king, served as a shepherd over his father's flocks and was God's choice to shepherd His people.

> You will shepherd my people Israel and become their ruler. (2 Samuel 5:2)
>
> He chose David his servant and took him from the sheep pens; from tending the sheep he brought him to be the shepherd of his people Jacob, of Israel his inheritance. David shepherded them with integrity of heart; with skillful hands he led them. (Psalm 78:70–71)

The Twenty-Third Psalm is one of the better-known texts of scripture and was authored by David. Each line of this beloved psalm revealed the love, care, and protection provided by the shepherd. David knew how to love and protect the flock. And he knew that God would love and protect him too, that Yahweh would be his Shepherd.

In 2 Samuel 12, we read about Nathan confronting David by telling the story of a ewe lamb that was brazenly taken from its owner and then slaughtered for a meal. King David, the shepherd-king, was furious that someone would do such a thing. Nathan told the allegory to get David to recognize his sin regarding Bathsheba and her husband. Although David was a victorious warrior, a wise king, and a great leader, there were times in his life when he was not the shepherd Israel needed. Just ask Uriah.

The Prophets Spoke of Israel's Shepherds

Some of the strongest references to shepherds as spiritual leaders are found in the writings of the prophets. God wasn't always pleased with those who served His people as shepherds, and the prophets were called to rebuke them. Ezekiel is a strong example. During his season of prophetic service, God was unhappy with Israel's shepherds. From Ezekiel 34, we learn of their displeasing behaviors:

- They cared only for themselves and not the flock (v. 2).

- They didn't help the weak (v. 4).

- They didn't heal their wounds or bind up the injured (v. 4).

- They didn't search for or bring back the lost sheep (v. 4).

- They were harsh and brutal with the sheep (v. 4).

These men didn't shepherd Israel in the manner God had had required of them; they failed the flock, leaving them vulnerable, sick, and lost. As a result, the scripture refers [at times] to Israel being sheep without a shepherd, or the lost sheep of Israel.

> Then Micaiah answered, "I saw all Israel scattered on the hills like sheep without a shepherd." (1 Kings 22:17)

> My people have been lost sheep; their shepherds have led them astray and caused them to roam on the mountains, they wandered over mountain and hill and forgot their own resting place. (Jeremiah 50:6)

> So they were scattered because there was no shepherd, and when they were scattered they became food for all the wild animals. My sheep wandered over all the mountains and on every high hill. They were scattered over the whole earth, and no one searched or looked for them. (Ezekiel 34:5–8)

The Messiah As the Shepherd of Israel

Due to His displeasure with Israel's shepherds, God declared that He would return to become their shepherd

(Ezekiel 34:5–16). That was a strong metaphor of the coming Messiah, of the Shepherd who would one day provide loving care for the flock. The Shepherd would gather Israel's scattered sheep from among the nations, restoring them by bringing them home.

> He tends his flock like a shepherd: He gathers the
> lambs in his arms and carries them close to his heart;
> he gently leads those that have young. (Isaiah 40:11)

God knew that no man of Israel could ever be the true and righteous king the people needed, could ever be the true shepherd of Israel. He knew the people would need a better shepherd, one of divine origin. By showing the people that their shepherds would ultimately fail, He was revealing two important lessons:

1. A shepherd selected from among the people could never succeed.

2. The shepherd they really needed could only come from Yahweh.

As the flocks were dependent on someone caring for them, so the people depended on a spiritual leader, a true pastor, a loving shepherd. The Hebrew text beautifully depicted the relationship God desired with Israel. That picture grows in significance as we look to Jesus, the Good Shepherd, and see the relationship he seeks to have with us.

From the Greek Text

It's no wonder that Jesus, the son of David, spoke so openly of the shepherd-sheep relationship. The Jews of his day were immersed in "flock" culture and were well acquainted with the stories and lessons from scripture. Jesus often illustrated his teaching using the symbols of sheep, goats, and shepherds; it was a common theme for him.

Did Jesus's emphasis on flocks and shepherds originate with him? Was this topic unique to Jesus? No, as we've seen, the emphasis of shepherds and flocks was rooted in the Old Testament. Let's take a closer look at some of the ways that Jesus fulfilled the role of the messianic Shepherd:

- He finds the lost sheep: "I have come to seek and to save that which is lost" (Luke 19:10).

- He dedicates his life to the flock: "For I have come not to be served, but to serve, and to give my life as ransom for many" (Mark 10:45).

- He leads them to water: "If anyone is thirsty come to me drink" (John 7:37).

- He knows them by name: "He calls his own sheep by name and leads them out" (John 10:3).

- He fulfills their needs: "I am the gate; whoever enters through me will be saved. They will come in and go out, and find pasture" (John 10:9).

- He protects them: "I am the good shepherd. The good shepherd lays his life down for the sheep" (John 10:11).

Sheep without a Shepherd

Jesus described his mission as that of a shepherd. More specifically, that he was the Shepherd of Israel, the promised Messiah. He knew that many of his people were lost sheep.

> Jesus went through all the towns and villages, teaching in their synagogues, preaching the good news of the kingdom and healing every disease and sickness.

> When he saw the crowds, he had compassion on them, because they were harassed and helpless, like sheep without a shepherd. Then he said to his disciples, "The harvest is plentiful but the workers are few. Ask the Lord of the Harvest, therefore, to send out workers into his harvest field."(Matthew 9:35–38)

Jesus was very specific about the spiritual condition of the crowds. Consider the two words he used:

> *Harassed.* The root for this Greek word has the idea of "flaying, to flay, which is to peel off the skin." Its wider usage suggests "the idea of trouble, to have trouble or to be in trouble."

> *Helpless.* The root for this Greek word carries the "idea of a quick movement, or quick motion of the hand, as in flicking something off you, such as dust or a piece of lint."

This isn't an action requiring focused thought, as would be the case in throwing a baseball. No, this is a quick movement of the hand to get something off your sleeve or to flick something off your shoe.

Jesus saw the "harassed and helpless" people. He had compassion for them because they were in trouble, as if someone had casually, and indifferently, flicked them off. The implication is that the shepherds who should have been caring for them had chosen not to, as if these crowds had been wiped off the bottom of a shoe. Sheep without a shepherd would be devoured, as if having their skin flayed off.

Why would sheep be without a shepherd? One possibility is that they have wandered off and the shepherds aren't looking for them. Another is that the shepherds didn't want the sheep. The tone of Jesus's words suggested that the people were in trouble because no one was helping them. Had those responsible for helping them chosen not to? The lost sheep were at risk, and no one seemed to care but Jesus.

Jesus Seeks and Saves the Lost Sheep

So who were those lost "unshepherded" people? Matthew 9 is an interesting chapter, revealing one example after another of people who were regarded as lost or unwanted. Here is a list of people in Matthew 9 who would be unclean and unwanted:

1. A paralyzed man (vv. 1–8)
2. A tax collector (vv. 9–13)
3. The disciples regarded as unfit, as if unqualified (vv. 14–17)
4. A dead girl (vv. 18–23)
5. A sick woman with a bleeding disorder (vv. 14–17)
6. Two blind men (vv. 27–31)
7. A demon-possessed man (vv. 32–34)
8. The sick and diseased crowds (vv. 35)

One way or another, those people in Matthew 9 were considered defiled (Leviticus 17). They would not be sought out for flock membership. The fact that they were sick, diseased, or demon-possessed was the key for why they were "lost sheep." Remember the disciples' question to Jesus in John 9:1: "Rabbi, who sinned, this man or his parents that he was born blind?" The Jews viewed the sick, diseased, and demon-possessed as sinners and, therefore, as unwanted sheep.

Israel's leaders often misunderstood the Messiah. Was their misunderstanding at least partially responsible for them not being better shepherds? The Messiah's enemies often accused him of cavorting with tax collectors and sinners, of casting out demons by the power of Satan, of abandoning their sacred traditions, of blasphemy, and many other charges (John 8:48; Luke 5:27–39, ch. 7). His detractors had issues with his allowing a sinful woman to touch him as Mary did when she washed his feet (Luke 7). The people were bothered when he entered Zacchaeus's house (Luke 19), or when he dined with Matthew and the other tax collectors and sinners (Luke 5). The religious ones charged with shepherding the people of Israel were angry when he forgave a lame man his sins (Luke 5). These accusations were most often made when he was helping those who had been flicked and wiped off.

Unclean and Unwanted

Certainly Jesus respected the Law of Moses regarding purity laws and commandments relating to being clean and undefiled. There are examples of his instructing the people he healed to show themselves to the priest (Matthew 8:4, Luke 17:14). The priest would pronounce them clean, thereby clearing them to return to temple to offer sacrifices for their cleansing. Jesus didn't break the law; he lived his life by the principles and values of what the Father intended the law to mean. When he touched a leper, he wasn't flaunting the Jews' purity laws; he was demonstrating love for his neighbor. When he cast out demons, it wasn't by the prince of demons but by the power of the Holy Spirit. When he touched lepers, healed the blind, or gave hearing to the deaf, it wasn't Jesus ignoring the laws of Moses but his fulfilling Isaiah 53:4: "He took up our infirmities and carried our diseases."

At the close of Matthew 9, Jesus asked his disciples to pray, and it was a specific prayer request—that the Lord of the harvest would send more workers into the harvest field. This is an interesting metaphor. The field, in its most obvious context, would be a grainfield, either barley or wheat. Praying to the Lord of the harvest suggested it was harvesttime, but there were not enough workers for the ingathering. I believe the symbolism is that the lost sheep needed harvesting too, that the disciples should pray, asking God to send out more shepherds into the harvest fields of lost lambs.

In his heart, Jesus was a shepherd, the Good Shepherd. His purpose was to care for all the sheep, to find those who were lost, and lovingly return them to the fold. He said, "For I have come to seek and to save that which is lost." Jesus came for the lost sheep of Israel, the unwanted, unclean, and the undesirable.

Sheep and Goats

On my third trip to Israel, I wanted to learn more about shepherds and their flocks. One day, my guide and I were driving back to Jerusalem when we came upon a large flock of sheep on a hillside close to the road. He pulled over, and I got out so I could watch the shepherd. His flocks had both sheep and goats. The sheep stayed together, close to the shepherd, grazing on what little there was to eat. The goats were also grazing, but they were roaming all around the area, on the outer edges of the flock. The goats didn't group together or stay huddled up like a flock of sheep; they each went their own way, following their own path. And they seemed to ignore the shepherd. I didn't understand the words he spoke, but the sheep did. It was his voice, the tone, and the gentle manner with which he spoke that made an impression on me. The sheep knew what he was saying. He was more assertive with the goats. They were always pressing the boundaries. As we drove off, I left with the sense that the shepherd would be out there all day. He would be watching, providing, and protecting his sheep, but I wondered about the goats.

The Flocks on Judgment Day

In Matthew 25, Jesus spoke of judgment day. He spoke of God separating the nations into two groups: the sheep on his right and the goats on his left. The basic idea—goats are stubbornly independent, and sheep are meekly submissive. The sheep will be gathered for eternal blessings, and the goats will be gathered for the other thing.

How is this to be measured? Jesus taught in Matthew 25 that the sheep are those who served the least among the flock: the sick, diseased, imprisoned, and homeless, the people who could not meet their own needs. These "least ones" were the ones who were lost and unwanted, having no one to help them. The goats were those who had seen the needs of the least, the lost ones, but had chosen not to help. Metaphorically, do goats simply wipe off the lost sheep from their shoes or simply flick them off their sleeves?

The Good Shepherd

The shepherd as a symbol proved to be a powerful metaphor for Jesus, our Messiah. We can more fully appreciate his loving care and embrace him with greater devotion by understanding his dedication to his flock.

From the creation of the world, God knew that his people would need a shepherd. From Adam to Malachi,

He knew the patriarchs, judges, priests, and kings would never be enough. We were always going to need the Good Shepherd who would one day lay down his life for us. The Good Shepherd would bring us through the new birth. He would fill our hunger and thirst for righteousness, protect us from the evil one and, when our time came, would carry us home. God knew that a shepherd would stand in for Abram, his descendants, and for us in the blood path to fulfill the blood covenant. Thank you, Jesus.

For Us Today

Many years ago, when my wife and I were newlyweds, an older couple from church, that we didn't know well, invited us to go on an overnight fishing trip. They had a farm just outside of town where they had lived all their lives. Everybody in town seemed to know them and were on a first-name basis. He was retired, having farmed and raised sheep for over fifty years. The fishing trip sounded like a good way to get to know them better, so off we went.

On arrival, we set up camp, got the boat in the water, and sat quietly while he patiently coaxed the motor into starting. The poor thing sounded like it was in the final throes of life. But it was a glorious afternoon of fishing, and in spite of the puttering, sputtering, barely running motor, we still caught a mess of fish and then headed in for dinner.

Later, after some excellent fried trout, our host said, "Come on, Brother Rick, let's go fishing before the sun goes down." So after working another motor miracle, we slowly cruised to the middle of the lake. He eased off the throttle and turned off the motor, to which I thought, *I sure hope he's got one more miracle.* So there we were, two men in a boat, watching the sun beginning to set. We didn't touch the poles, didn't bait a hook. We weren't there to fish.

It turned out that our hosts were in a crisis about the church and were considering leaving. They weren't lost sheep exactly, but they were crowding the edges. You could say they felt harassed and helpless and, perhaps, cast out, like sheep without a flock. Their crisis stemmed from a painful church division. Some eighteen months prior to my serving as their preaching minister, an acrimonious split erupted with 150 members leaving to start their own congregation. The issues aren't relevant to my story, except to say that this older couple didn't understand the issues. But they were certainly brokenhearted over it. They tried attending worship at both congregations, alternating Sundays, but that didn't last. They gave effort to getting the groups to reunite, but it was not to be. This was why they invited us to the lake, why he and I were out there at dusk.

After a few moments, his chin dropped, he sighed heavily and began to cry. From his broken heart and with tear-filled eyes, he asked, "Rick, why do churches tear themselves apart?" I was totally unprepared for the question. I had no insightful comments, no wisdom to offer, and nothing with which to ease his pain. I was twenty-six years old, with no experience in church conflicts. The only thing I thought to say was, "I don't know, but they do, and it's terribly sad." He only nodded. And then the conversation took a different turn.

He raised his head, looked at me with laser-beam intensity, and told me his story. For most of his life, he had been a shepherd, raising sheep and caring for flocks for over fifty years. He shared the stories of his shepherding experiences. He spoke of the lambing season, of how he would get little or no sleep for days at a time. He took such special care of the lambs, especially for those that were born in distress. He talked about all he did to save them, to keep them alive. There were stories of great joy and of terrible sadness. He protected the flock, provided for them, and worried about them. It was obvious that he loved being a shepherd. Caring for the flock was such a huge part of him, of who and what he was in life. The longer he talked, the more I understood what he was doing and why he was telling his story. Finally it ended. He gathered himself, went to work on the motor, and with another miracle, it started. Before getting us back to shore, he asked one more question, "Rick, why can't church elders be true shepherds of the flock?"

From the mouth of a shepherd came a question I've never forgotten. Sheep need a shepherd who will lay his life down for them. If he won't, he isn't really a shepherd; he's just something else.

Our Shepherd is committed to us. He knows. He understands. He provides and protects. At times, we feel alone, vulnerable, and lost. If so, he will find us. If we are afraid, he will calm our fears. If we hunger and thirst, he will fill us with righteousness. If we are hurt, he will bind our wounds.

Sheep, shepherds, and goats—from the Hebrew scriptures, we glimpse their history and their role among God's people. From there, the text moves us forward to Jesus, our Messiah, the shepherd the world really needed.

> I am the good shepherd. The good shepherd lays
> down his life for the sheep.
>
> —John 10:11

8

The Big Rock Religion of Caesarea Philippi

There are places in this world that evoke a feeling of fear and evil or have a sense of being dark and dangerous. Some people feel that way in cemeteries, especially at night. Others get a sense of foreboding when entering old, abandoned houses or buildings. Most of us would choose not to buy a house built over a cemetery or a house where the previous owners were murdered. To put it bluntly, some places just give us the creeps.

Few places evoke an evil response quite as strong as the ancient ruins of Paneas. Each time I visit there, I get a sense of being in the presence of evil. The ancient city of Paneas is roughly twenty-three miles north of the Sea of Galilee. Bible readers will know the city by its more common name: Caesarea Philippi. In 20 BC, the region of Panion was assimilated into the kingdom of Herod the Great. In 2 BC, Philip, Herod's son, founded the city of Paneas; and in AD 14, with Rome's permission, he renamed the city Caesarea, in honor of Caesar Augustus. It became known as Caesarea Philippi to distinguish the city from his father's home, Caesarea Maritima, on the Mediterranean coast.

The Fertility God Pan

Caesarea Philippi (CP) was famous for its temples and worship to the fertility god Pan. The half-man, half-goat idol was celebrated as the god of wild nature, herdsmen, and music.[1] Being a god of music, he was portrayed playing a flute, the pan flute. The purpose of worshiping Pan was to seek his favors in the form of rain for the crops, flocks, and herds, and for human fertility as well.

The worship practices were pagan through and through. The celebrations were disgusting and decadent and, therefore, popular among the people of the region. The priests of Pan served in the temple and facilitated the annual festival of Pan, which included, among other things, a community-wide orgy. The priests copulated in a wide variety of ways: with heterosexual and homosexual pairings, pedophilia, and bestiality.[2]

> Pan was depicted as an ugly man with the horns, legs, and ears of a goat. Most stories about him refer to sexual affairs. The worship practices of his followers were no different. Pan was associated with Dionysus, the Greek god of wine and orgies, whose worshipers continued many of the sexual rites of the Old Testament gods of the Baal cult. Dionysus was worshiped in the pagan Decapolis across the Sea of Galilee from the center of Jesus' ministry. Clearly, though the names of the gods had changed, the people's worship practices had not.[3]

Jesus Among the Gentiles

So it seems strange that Jesus would purposely go to Caesarea Philippi and take his young disciples with him. The question of *why* begs to be asked. Why intentionally leave the borders of northern Israel and travel to a Gentile region known for its pagan and defiling practices? It's unimaginable that Jesus would take his disciples to this horrible place. Whatever the reason, the fact remains that Jesus took them there, and the Rabbi always had a reason.

Would this be the only time Jesus ventured outside the borders of his country? If there are other instances, how do they harmonize with his commitment of going only to the lost sheep of Israel? The exploration of these questions requires us to first go back to Abraham and the prophets. Was there a vision or prophecy for the Messiah to go to the Gentiles? We know, of course, that the Gospel was always meant for the world, and salvation would be offered to all nations. But was it prophesied that Messiah, during his earthly ministry, would venture outside of Israel and go among the pagans? Was it prophesied that he would reach out to the non-Jewish world?

From the Hebrew Text

What Did the Prophets Say About the Messiah and Gentiles?

Consider the following texts:

- "All the nations of the earth shall be blessed through you" (Genesis 12:3).

- "Abraham will surely become a great and powerful nation, and all nations on earth will be blessed through him" (Genesis 18:18).

- "The people walking in darkness have seen a great light; on those living in the land of deep darkness a light has dawned" (Isaiah 9:2).

- "I, the Lord, have called you in righteousness; I will take hold of your hand. I will keep you and will make you to be a covenant for the people and a light for the Gentiles" (Isaiah 42:6).

- "I will also make you a light for the Gentiles that my salvation may reach to the ends of the earth" (Isaiah 49:6).

- "Arise, shine, for your light has come, and the glory of the Lord rises upon you. See, darkness covers the earth and thick darkness is over the peoples; but the Lord rises upon you and his glory appears over you. Nations will come to your light, and kings to the brightness of your dawn" (Isaiah 60:1–3).

The prophets carried a consistent message regarding how the Gentile nations would one day flow to Mount Zion. But the prophecies envisioned the Messiah restoring Israel first and defeating their Gentile enemies. Then—and only then—would the kingdom be open to the nations. The expectations of the Jews were that the Gentiles would embrace Judaism, the Law of Moses, and Jewish customs.

It's easier to imagine the Son of Man seeking and saving the lost as long as the lost were Israel's scattered sheep. The idea of his reaching out to the Gentiles before Israel's restoration would have seemed somehow wrong or, at the very least, unlikely. The prophets looked forward to the coming Messiah and prophesied that the nations would flow to him. He would be a banner to the nations and their kings. He would be a light to those living in darkness. The nations and their kings coming to the Messiah was always the plan of God, but it was only going to happen after the restoration of Israel.

From the Greek Text

Messiah's kingdom was never going to have overpowering military strength, unimaginable wealth, or far reaching political power. It was to be a kingdom of conscience and divine character. His kingdom would be about humility, sacrifice, and service and would call both Jews and Gentiles to live under Messiah's banner.

Jesus came to earth with full knowledge of his mission and with a surrendered heart to his Father's will. What was his prayer in the garden? "Not my will but yours be done." Yes, the Messiah's mission was to return the lost sheep of Israel to the flock of God. But that flock would one day include the sheep living in darkness. It would be a global kingdom available to all believers: "For God so loved the world that he gave his one and only son that whoever believed would not die but have everlasting life" (John 3:16).

The challenge came after the Gospel began spreading outside of Israel to the Gentiles, free of charge, which is to say, without Judaism attached. There had always been room in Judaism for Gentiles, providing the men were circumcised, embraced the Law of Moses, and followed Jewish customs. The temple had a Court of the Gentiles for a reason. Offering the kingdom of God to the Gentiles by grace and without the law was heresy to most Christian Jews. But that is what Jesus came to offer, a relationship with God by grace and mercy. The New Covenant was a covenant of the Spirit. A covenant relationship with God through Messiah is offered to all people, to all nations, in all times zones.

> Now the Lord is the Spirit, and where the Spirit of the Lord is, there is freedom. And we all, who with

> unveiled faces contemplate the Lord's glory, are being
> transformed into his image with ever-increasing glory,
> which comes from the Lord, who is the Spirit. (2
> Corinthians 3:17–18)

Jesus interacted with Gentiles. He intentionally went outside of Israel's borders, planting the seeds for global salvation, offering hope to those living in darkness. So it shouldn't surprise us to see Jesus traveling to the regions across the Jordan, or to Tyre and Sidon, to Samaria, or to the region of Caesarea Philippi. Let's take a closer look at Jesus's Gentile interactions.

The Region of the Gadarenes

The area of the Gadarenes, also known as Gergesenes or Gerasenes, was part of the region across the Jordan River known as the Decapolis (this was Greek, *deca* for "ten" and *polis* for "city"). The Decapolis was the ten city-states established by Alexander the Great. They were pagan and Gentile.

Obviously, a herd of pigs, or even one pig, would be unclean for Jews. But Jesus chose to come near a heard of pigs and used his power to heal two men, two gentile men.

> When he arrived at the other side in the region of
> the Gadarenes, two demon-possessed men coming
> from the tombs met him. They were so violent that
> no one could pass that way. "What do you want with
> us, Son of God?" they shouted. "Have you come
> here to torture us before the appointed time?" Some
> distance from them a large herd of pigs was feeding.
> The demons begged Jesus, "If you drive us out, send us
> into the herd of pigs." He said to them, "Go!" So they
> came out and went into the pigs, and the whole herd

rushed down the steep bank into the lake and died in the water.

Those tending the pigs ran off, went into the town and reported all this, including what had happened to the demon-possessed men. Then the whole town went out to meet Jesus. And when they saw him, they pleaded with him to leave their region. (Matthew 8:28–34)

The demons knew who Jesus was and suggested that he was somehow out of sync, by being among the Gentiles and unclean animals. They didn't expect him to be in the Decapolis, didn't expect him to limit their power. By casting them out of the men, Jesus demonstrated that he was Lord of all and that he cared for everyone and that the time would come when he will bless all people.

Into Tyre and Sidon

For Abraham's descendants, the land of Canaan was the land of milk and honey. But Canaan was also known as the land of the seven pagan nations (Deuteronomy 7:1). In Genesis 10:19, we learn that Sidon was one of the northern borders of Canaan. Jacob declared in Genesis 49:13 that Zebulon and his people would live by the seashore and his border will extend toward Sidon. During Solomon's reign, he created an alliance with the king of Tyre, agreeing to give him villages in Galilee in exchange for materials for his construction projects in Jerusalem (1 Kings 9:11). During the divided kingdom, Tyre and Sidon gained power and strength.

Do you remember Jezebel? She was a Sidonian princess and the wife of Jerobaom, king of Israel. Jezebel was hugely influential in introducing idol worship to Israel, especially Baal worship. There was much history between the two coastal cities and the people of Israel. Then one day, hundreds of years later, Jesus of Nazareth decided to go to the coast. He went specifically to the region of Tyre and Sidon——and had an encounter with a Canaanite woman, a Gentile.

> Leaving that place, Jesus withdrew to the region of Tyre and Sidon. A Canaanite woman from that vicinity came to him crying out, "Lord, Son of David, have mercy on me! My daughter is suffering terribly from demon-possession." Jesus did not answer a word. So his disciples came to him and urged him, "Send her away, for she keeps crying out after us." He answered, "I was sent only to the lost sheep of Israel." The woman came and knelt before him. "Lord, help me!" she said. He replied, "It is not right to take the children's bread and toss it to their dogs." "Yes, Lord," she said, "but even the dogs eat the crumbs that fall from their master's table." Then Jesus answered, "Woman, you have great faith! Your request is granted." And her daughter was healed from that very hour. (Matthew 15:21–28)

The Canaanite woman knew who Jesus was and believed he came to help her. The metaphor Jesus used in the conversation was startling. Much attention is paid to the part where Jesus told her that it isn't right to give bread to dogs. Was he inferring that she was a dog? Was he intentionally diminishing her as a person because she was a Gentile? I don't believe so. But he was testing her faith. Once she demonstrated true faith, then Jesus was willing to grant her request. This was faith triumphing over heritage. The test was whether she truly believed in Jesus or was holding on to the beliefs with which she was raised.

The reference to his being sent to the lost sheep of Israel was really interesting. Why was Jesus in her region? If he was searching for Israel's lost sheep, then he went to Tyre and Sidon in search of Jews who were lost, to Jewish people separated from the flock by life's circumstances. Was this woman one of Israel's lost sheep? But she was a Canaanite woman and not a lost sheep of Israel. Was the bread reserved for only the lost Jews? Did Jesus have the vision and compassion to see Gentiles as lost sheep as well?

The Messiah came for everyone, to call the nations, to offer them grace. He used his divine power to heal the woman's daughter, to cast out the demon. Try to imagine what this would mean to her personally, as a mother and as a Gentile.

However this fascinating text is to be understood, at the very least, it illustrates our Savior going outside of Israel to help and heal others in need.

Jesus Visits Samaria—Twice

The Jewish-Samaritan conflict began some six centuries prior to the time of Jesus's public ministry. The conflict was rooted in events surrounding the Assyrian conquest and exile of most of the Jews in Israel during the divided kingdom. Shortly after the second Assyrian exile, in 606 BC, Assyria's king sent Gentiles from five countries into Israel to manage the Jews who were left behind. Soon those Gentile managers married local Jewish women, and over time, the population of Jewish-Gentile marriages and families increased. When the Jews of the southern kingdom of Judah, who were exiled to Babylon, began returning to their homeland, they encountered this mixed breed living in the region. The pure blooded Jews returning to Judea felt resentment and hatred, and soon had conflict with the Samaritans.

However, Jesus wasn't interested in the old hatreds and prejudices. As a rabbi, he pushed the boundaries of propriety when he used a "Samaritan man" in one of his better-known parables, the parable of the good Samaritan. He wouldn't reference the Samaritan in a negative way. In fact, in this parable, the Samaritan is painted as a man more righteous than a Jewish priest or a Levite (Luke 10:25–37).

As we will see in the John 4 text, Jews did not associate with Samaritans, and the two cultures certainly didn't worship together.

First visit into Samaria

> Now he had to go through Samaria. So he came to a town in Samaria called Sychar, near the plot of ground Jacob had given to his son Joseph. Jacob's well was there, and Jesus, tired as he was from the journey, sat down by the well. It was at the sixth hour. When a Samaritan woman came to draw water, Jesus said to her, "Will you give me a drink?" His disciples had gone into town to buy food. The Samaritan woman said to him, "You are a Jew and I am a Samaritan woman. How can you ask me for a drink?" For Jews do not associate with Samaritans. (John 4:1–9)

How surprising it must have been for the disciples to have their rabbi lead them into Samaria. Why would he do that? The Messiah wanted to go to Samaria and chose to do so, twice. The Samarians were also lost sheep to Jesus.

As a matter of course, Jews would not travel through Samaria. To do so would make them unclean and defiled. The Samaritans were sandwiched in between the Jews, with Galilee above them and Judea below. The Samaritans wouldn't have traveled into either place. As John recorded, "For Jews do not associate with Samaritans." That Jesus would choose to go there is remarkable. The text records in John 4:4, "Now he had to go through Samaria." This statement was made in the context of verses 1–3, where Jesus decided it was time for him to leave Judea and go back to Galilee.

The Jews had a route for traveling between Judea and Galilee, but it circumvented Samaria. A typical route from Jerusalem would be to go East and down to Jericho, then turn north at the Jordan River, until they had bypassed Samaria, and then back west into Galilee. Jesus didn't have to go into Samaria because there was no other way. The necessity for going came from a higher place with a greater purpose.

Going into Samaria was prophetic; it was messianic. However, I can find no specific text prophesying that the Messiah would go into Samaria. But his messianic mission was to seek the lost sheep of Israel. I believe that, for Jesus, the Samaritans were also sons of Abraham. They were lost and in the darkness. So Jesus, on two different occasions, chose to go into Samaria to find those who believed in him and to bring them back to the flock of God. Most of the Jews wouldn't have considered the Samaritans as lost sheep of Israel, but Jesus did. He connected with this woman at Jacob's well and offered her the gift of Living Water. Jesus, in John 7, offered Living Water to all who believed in him. John recorded that Jesus was referring to the Holy Spirit, whom those who believed would later receive (Joel 2:28–32 and Acts 2:1–33).

The Samaritan woman was convicted that Jesus was the Messiah, and she went back to her village to tell everyone that she had found Him (John 3:28–30). The result was that many in the village of Sychar believed in Jesus. In fact, the Samaritans urged him to stay a few more days, and he did! Again, imagine the impact on his disciples when they learned that Jesus intended to stay in Sychar, in Samaria, for several more days. The Samaritans were the people the Jews loved to hate. For a few days, the disciples had a bird's-eye view of their rabbi reaching out to the great unwashed and inviting them to rejoin the flock of God.

Second visit into Samaria

> As time approached for him to be taken up to heaven, Jesus resolutely set out for Jerusalem, and he sent messengers on ahead. They went into a Samaritan village to get things ready for him, but the people there did not welcome him, because he was heading for Jerusalem. When the disciples James and John saw this, they asked, 'Lord, do you want us to call fire down from heaven to destroy them?' But Jesus turned and rebuked them, and they went to another village. (Luke 9:51–56)

We see the disciples' attitude toward the Samaritans in Jesus's second visit to Samaria. The Luke 9 text indicated that his time had come, and so he set his face toward Jerusalem, to Passover and Golgotha. He led his disciples through Samaria instead of around it. They came to a village, but this time, the people didn't respond in faith or welcome him; so some of his disciples, highly offended, asked Jesus the following question: "Lord, do you want us to call down fire from heaven to destroy them?" (Luke 9:54). Jesus turned and rebuked them.

Sometimes we want to "destroy" others, to see them suffer for their actions and attitudes. Jesus's life and ministry were constant reminders that his kingdom was a place of humility, compassion, and forgiveness. Jesus did not want fire called down to burn every man, woman, and child of Sychar. Should we?

Jesus's message wasn't determined by geography—as in Jerusalem versus Samaria. It wasn't built on who possessed the greater claim to sacred ground—as in Jacob's well versus the temple. Nor was it determined by gender, race, or even theology. This was Jesus of Nazareth, the Son of God, the Son of David, offering the woman and her village the gift of Living Water. Two thousand years later, the same Living Water is still offered. He offered it to me, a Gentile.

Going to the House of Pan: Caesarea Philippi

As mentioned above, Caesarea Philippi was devoted to the worship of Pan, a fertility god. There were many fertility gods in the first century, but this town was about the half-man, half-goat god that blessed the conception of babies, animals, and crops.

There was a hill or a small mountain with a vertical rock face rising maybe one hundred feet in height. Carved into the face of the rock were a series of niches that housed the statues of Pan's nymphs, his wives. To the far left of the rock wall was a cave, out from which flowed a river. Through the centuries, geological shifts have rerouted the water that runs out of the cave; it is now far less in volume. In the first-century pagan world, it was believed that water—lakes, rivers, —were portals to the underworld. The spirits and gods came up from the underworld through water to enter the realm of men. The Pan worshipers believed that the goat god would come up from the underworld through the river and emerge out of the cave to copulate with his wives, pouring his seed on the land in the form of rain. Chiseled into the face of the rock was the largest niche that housed a statue of Pan.

This is the idea of the big rock religion of Caesarea Philippi. It was here, to the region of CP, that Jesus brought his disciples. Talk about your lost sheep! Those Pan worshipers weren't descendants of Abraham. They were not even the mixed bloodlines of Jews and Gentiles. None of this mattered to Jesus. He traveled to the region and took his disciples with him.

> When Jesus came to the region of Caesarea Philippi, he asked his disciples, "Who do people say the Son of Man is?" They replied, "Some say John the Baptist; others say Elijah; and still others, Jeremiah or one of the prophets." "But what about you?" he asked. "Who do you say I am?" Simon Peter answered, "You are the Christ, the Son of the living God." Jesus answered, "Blessed are you, Simon son of Jonah, for this was not revealed to you by man, but by my Father in heaven. And I tell you that you are Peter, and on this rock I will build my church, and the gates of Hades will not overcome it." (Matthew 16:13–20)

I believe that the rock Jesus would build on was a symbol with double meaning. The first symbol was the rock of his divinity. The second symbol of the rock was his church being built at Caesarea Philippi. Was he using the shrines as a metaphor for global evangelism? Was Jesus mentoring his disciples by calling them to make disciples of the pagan goat worshipers?

This was the kingdom to which the disciples would receive keys. Keys either lock or unlock. I can believe that if Jesus was talking with the twelve and they were in sight of the rock, his disciples having keys would have greater impact. Assuming that his disciples went back to preach the Gospel in Caesarea Philippi, the Father would honor what they did with their keys.

Is this why Jesus said that the gates of Hades would not stand? The disciples' keys are greater than those used in the pagan world. The reason the gates of Hades stood closed was to keep the forces of light from going through. Jesus gave his wide-eyed followers a greater vision. Hade's gate would not stand; it would not stop the forces of righteousness. Jesus would send them to make disciples of all nations in all places of the earth. He would send them to Caesarea Philippi and to its pagan people with their heathen beliefs.

Does Caesarea Philippi seem like the place Isaiah had in mind when he wrote the following?

- "In the past he humbled the land of Zebulun and the land of Naphtali, but in the future he will honor Galilee of the Gentiles, by the way of the sea, along the Jordan. The people walking in darkness have seen a great light; on those living in the land of darkness a light has dawned" (Isaiah 9:1–2).

- "I, the Lord, have called you in righteousness; I will take hold of your hand. I will keep you and will make you to be a covenant for the people and a light for the Gentiles, to open eyes that are blind, to free captives from prison and to release from the dungeon those who sit in darkness" (Isaiah 42:6–7).

- "He says, 'It is too small a thing for you to be my servant to restore the tribes of Jacob and bring back those of Israel I have kept. I will also make you

> a light for the Gentiles, that you may bring my
> salvation to the ends of the earth'" (Isaiah 49:6).

Jesus very intentionally traveled to the Decapolis and into the region of Tyre and Sidon, to Samaria, and to the region of Caesarea Philippi. He fulfilled Isaiah's messianic prophecies. Consider some of his phrasing "those living in darkness have seen a great light" and "to release from the dungeon those who sit in darkness" and "that you may bring my salvation to the ends of the earth." What can we say but, "Wow, what a Savior!"

For Us Today

Is it un-Messiah-like to go around pointing out the Gentiles? Biblically, everyone not born of Jewish parents is a Gentile. But if the word is used as a metaphor for anyone different, offensive, or unwanted, then who are the Gentiles? Does America have its versions of Tyre, Sidon, Sychar, or even Caesarea Philippi? Do we have places we loathe like Samaria or regions like the Decapolis? Are there states, cities, or even organizations that we think of in less-than-glowing terms? What about individuals? Do believers sometimes say disparaging things about other people? Are some of us in the habit of assigning Gentile status to others just because we want to?

I have witnessed attitudes and behaviors that diminish the human spirit, things that bring us down to that lower place. I've seen hatred, racism, and violence, and not just once or twice. Haven't you? People attack people over ideologies, customs, skin color, and sometimes just because they don't like them. Even within the body of Christ, I've witnessed behavior that I would have thought impossible. But it was, and it is.

I know of a Bible school teacher who refused to teach because a Vietnamese child was added to her class. "I don't teach gooks" was the complaint. I've heard racial jokes told while waiting for church to start. In one congregation, a deacon was telling a racial joke to a friend because a family of color was visiting for the first time and happened to sit right in front of them. They were the first African American family to visit our all-white church. I've even known brothers of the same family who hadn't spoken to each other in years; such was their animosity and pride.

So who are the Gentiles among us, they are anyone I don't like. If I feel entitled to discriminate and segregate, to hate and to keep hatred in my heart, then maybe I'm the Gentile. Anyway, none of this is Messiah-like.

All saved people become saved by God's good grace. Everyone started out broken by sin and flawed by sin's imperfection, for all have sinned and fallen short. But the blood of Jesus washes everyone's sin. At the end of the day, we're all Gentile sinners. None of us measures up to His glory. The ugliness of hatred, and prejudice must, at times, stretch the very fabric of God's patience.

Perhaps this story might help.

I got a call one morning from a member of my church. Her husband was in crisis and was in route to the emergency room. On arrival, I found him in the cardiac intensive care unit. Later that night, he would lose the battle. The family asked me to officiate his memorial service, which I was honored to do. But this included reaching out to their adult son, someone I had heard about but not met until that day at the hospital. Like me, he was raised in the church and, from birth, had attended with his family the congregation I then was serving as minister. However, he hadn't attended any worship services in a long time, or any church events;

in fact, he hadn't stepped foot in that church since he was a teenager.

One Sunday morning, he was sitting with a friend on a back row, and during the sermon, they were talking to each other. The preacher, irritated by their behavior, called out their names, and rebuked them. Feeling embarrassed and angry, the young man got up and walked out of the church and never came back. In fact, he hadn't been back until the day of his father's funeral some twenty-five years later. This was how and why we became friends. But it would take some time; for, to me, he was a Gentile.

He wasn't well. In fact, he was in treatment for an illness that would end his life in another six months. Not only was he sick but was also embroiled in legal difficulties. He lived under house arrest wearing an ankle bracelet. He had to get approval to go to his doctor's appointments and treatments, and he had to get approval to attend his dad's funeral.

In a few days following the service, he invited me to his house for coffee. I wasn't sure how I felt about it, but I agreed. But it was fine, and so we began meeting weekly and did so for several months, right up until he died. In our meetings, he found his words, and he wanted and needed to talk. We talked about our backgrounds, families, and common interests—the things people talk about when getting acquainted.

But after two or three weeks, he began to go deeper. He told me about his troubles, his arrest and pending trials. He was wrestling with the fact that he didn't have long to live. The conversations turned to the spiritual. He asked questions about God and grace, about heaven hell and forgiveness. He wondered if God honored the repentance of those who were close to their own end. He was a man rough around the edges, very rough, but underneath the hard exterior was a really good, but broken heart. It was a heart covered up by sin, anger, and bitterness. He felt guilty about what he had put his family through. He struggled with his mistakes and the bad choices. He doubted the wisdom of having walked out of church that Sunday morning. He was coming to grips with having turned his back on the Lord and on his spiritual heritage. He confessed his sins and his sinful life.

Saying it out loud to someone was helpful. Sometimes, while listening to him, I was in pain regarding the depth of his depravity. Some of his stories were heartbreaking and soul-wrenching.

He was, to me, a Gentile. He was so unclean, and defiled How awful of me, right? I know. You see, most of the time, the people I've led to the Lord have been relatively clean, decent, and law-abiding. Their sins have been small, unimpressive, just normal everyday kinds of sins, at least the ones they told me about. But not this man, this one came straight from Pan's cave. He was from the far side of the Jordan, from the the Decapolis. He was a Gentile.

One day, as we talked, he began weeping uncontrollably. We knelt down on the floor, and through his tears and anguish, he sought the mercy and grace of God. We wept and prayed together. Like the prodigal son, he begged his Father to forgive him and take him back. There have been few times that I have felt the presence and power of the Holy Spirit as vividly and as strong. We embraced each other as brothers in Christ. It was an incredible moment.

With the weeks he had left to live, he made the most of his time. He got his house arrest adjusted so he could attend worship with his family. After walking out twenty-five years earlier, he was now walking in every Sunday. There he was, down front with his family, singing and praising with all of his heart, happy and at peace. After a few precious weeks of renewed life, he was brought to that church for the last time. I grieved his death but celebrated his life restored to God. I still miss him and think of him often. And often wonder who was the Gentile in the story.

He taught me things I didn't know about myself. I didn't realize my self-righteousness, or how uncomfortable I was with people truly ravaged by sin. In the end, he taught me about Jesus and the willingness of God to give grace to those in need.

Yes, I love the idea of Jesus coming to serve and not to be served. As a Gentile, I consider myself blessed to be one of those Jesus came to serve. But in the context of two thousand years ago, when Jesus was seeking Israel's scattered sheep, my salvation seems hard to imagine. But then I read the prophets, of how the Messiah would reach out to those in the land of darkness. And I have hope.

Jesus went to the place of Pan. He didn't go there to eliminate those who were rooted in the big rock religion of Caesarea Philippi. He didn't notice the differences, the lines of separation. He simply saw lost sheep and a Father who longed for their return. Jesus came for the Pan worshipers and for people like my friend, and he came for me. Thank you, Jesus.

9

Saving a Wee Little Man

My parents were huge fans of Bible school, and they wanted their children to attend Bible classes every Sunday morning and Wednesday night, which we did, religiously. Bible school was held in classrooms organized by age or by grade. The average classroom was equipped with a bulletin board, a blackboard (which wasn't black but green) and a flannelgraph board, which was used for illustrating Bible stories. The illustrations were "paper doll" cutout figures and were backed with something that kept them stuck to the board. Flannelgraph represented the best technology of the day, at least for Bible school. I thought it was cool, and what else was there? The chalkboard was no competition. The flannel figures were brightly colored, and they were fun to look at. Welcome to Bible class in 1962.

Bible school, with its flannelgraph, was where I first learned about Zacchaeus, one of my all-time favorite stories found in Luke 19:1–10. There was even a fun little song that went with the story. If you aren't familiar, here are the lyrics:

> Zacchaeus was a wee little man, and a wee little man was he.
>
> He climbed up in a sycamore tree, for the savior to see.
>
> And as the savior walked that way, he looked up in that tree.

> And he said, "Zacchaeus, you come down, for I'm going to your house this day, for I'm going to your house this day."

The song had hand motions too. At the part about Zacchaeus being a "wee little man," we put our right hand a few inches above our left hand to illustrate how Zacchaeus was, in fact, a wee little man. To this day, I think of him as being four inches tall. The story of Zacchaeus, like the flannelgraph figures, stuck with me. Maybe it was the song, and maybe it was something else.

Looking at the figures on the flannel board, I was pretty sure I wanted to grow up tall, not wanting to be a wee little man. The average height of a first-century Jewish male was five foot one to five foot three, depending on the source.[1] Some suggest that Jesus was no more than five foot one,[2] but no one knows for sure. It's reasonable to think that he was between five feet one and five feet five inches tall. How tall would Zacchaeus have been to be considered short? Under five feet? In Luke 19:3, Zacchaeus was described as being short. In fact, the story is that he had to climb a tree since he couldn't see over the heads of the crowd.

All the people in the story thought he was a bad man, but I couldn't grasp why the people thought that, or why they were so unhappy with Jesus for going to his house. Nor was there any explanation to the words, "For this man too is a son of Abraham." Why did he need saving? And why did Jesus say that he came to seek and to save the lost? These questions were not addressed in Bible class.

I'm still reading his story and, yes, even singing the song, sans the hand motions. There are deeper things about the story that get my attention, for the story is actually quite powerful. Zacchaeus is a strong example of the Messiah's amazing mission and ministry. It's a story of salvation, offered to a man in desperate need of being saved. Zacchaeus made some different choices for a Jewish man. Those choices defined him, and they resulted in painful conflicts between him and his neighbors. By the story's end, the crowd was angry with Zacchaeus and not too happy with Jesus either. Jesus accepted Zacchaeus, sought fellowship with him, and offered salvation, none of which were popular with the crowd. We will explore the reasons for their angst and animosity. But first, here is his story:

> Jesus entered Jericho and was passing through. A man was there by the name of Zacchaeus; he was a chief tax collector and was wealthy. He wanted to see who Jesus was, but being a short man he could not, because of the crowd. So he ran ahead and climbed a sycamore-fig tree to see him, since Jesus was coming that way.
>
> When Jesus reached the spot, he looked up and said to him, "Zacchaeus, come down immediately. I must stay at your house today." So he came down and welcomed him gladly. All the people saw this and began to mutter, "He has gone to be the guest of a sinner."
>
> But Zacchaeus stood up and said to the Lord, "Look, Lord! Here and now I give half of my possessions to the poor, and if I have cheated anybody out of anything, I will pay back four times the amount."
>
> Jesus said to him, "Today salvation has come to this house, because this man, too, is a son of Abraham. For the Son of Man came to seek and to save what was lost." (Luke 19:1–10)

Grasping the greater meaning of this story requires a closer examination of the Law of Moses. Let's venture further back from Luke 19 to the teachings of Judaism. Let's seek to understand why the people considered Zacchaeus a sinner and why he was in need of salvation. If he was a son of Abraham, then how could he be lost? We will also review some of Israel's history leading up to the time and conditions in which Zacchaeus lived.

From the Hebrew Text

God's purpose for entering into a covenant relationship with the Hebrew people was clearly stated:

> Now if you obey me fully and keep my covenant, then out of all nations you will be my treasured possession. Although the whole earth is mine, you will be for me a kingdom of priests and a holy nation. (Exodus 19:5–6)

From the beginning, God sought a unique relationship with the Hebrews. They would become His holy nation, inheriting the Promise Land, following the Law of Moses, and honoring God with faith and obedience. He, in turn, would protect them, ensuring their success and prosperity and revealing to the nations around them that He, Yahweh, was the one true God. Holiness was a key factor in this relationship; God would consistently emphasize holiness to His people.

A Nation of Holiness

Consider these texts:

- "You are to be my holy people" (Exodus 22:31).
- "Therefore be holy, because I am holy" (Leviticus 11:45)
- "Be holy because I, the Lord your God, am holy" (Leviticus 19:1)

God wanted them to live differently from the nations surrounding them. They were to be set apart, sanctified for Him. The differences were noticeable. Holiness permeated every aspect of their lives. Here are some examples of what had to be kept holy:

- The temple, priesthood, and everything related to the sacrifices
- The food and the utensils used to prepare the food
- What they could touch and not touch
- Morality, sexuality, childbirth, family, and all aspects of daily life

Holiness Exchanged for Worldliness

In time, Israel traded being led by God to becoming a monarchy with a Jewish king on the throne. Thus began the 120 years of the united kingdom led by Saul, David, and Solomon. Due to an ever-diminishing desire for God's holiness, the kingdom collapsed, dissolving into the divided kingdom of Judah and Israel. Eventually, for reasons of rebellion and idolatry, they were exiled to Assyria and Babylon. Eventually, the descendants in Babylonian captivity returned home. By the first century AD, Israel was a nation with Judea to the south, Galilee to the north, and the two separated by Samaria in the middle—all ruled by Rome. It's the Palestine into which the Messiah was born.

The people were striving to keep Torah, to remain faithful to God's covenant, but Israel wasn't the nation they once were. Gone were the kingdoms of David's power and Solomon's splendor. Their greatest challenge was the absence of a Davidic descendant on the throne. Without a descendant of David as king, there could not be a free and independent Israel. Instead, they were a vassal territory of the Roman Empire and lived under the hard and heavy boot of Roman law. The temple continued, the priesthood served, and the daily sacrifices were honored. The Jews gathered to Jerusalem to observe the feasts. But it wasn't the same. Without the covenant of holiness and a son of David on the throne, Israel struggled to be little more than a slave state. They had become a nation of lost sheep, harassed and helpless, with nowhere to turn or anyone to turn to.

Living under Roman oppression, the people still had to survive, and they had to pay significant amounts of taxes and tribute to their masters. It wasn't easy. But there were new opportunities in Israel for making money, even to prosper. Doors opened for those willing to provide services and goods related to Roman interests.[3] Entire new trades developed, which were profitable but also placed the Jewish tradesmen in direct conflict with Mosaic law and its keepers. Much of the conflict related to issues of purity and the laws of ceremonial cleanliness and defilement. With a strange twist of irony, the issues of purity revolved around holiness, and holiness was the single greatest issue, which resulted in their ancestors falling into exile.

The Mosaic law and its endless traditions enforced holiness in first-century Palestine. The traditions got stapled to the law, which made them appear as if they were one and the same. The trouble came when the new commercial enterprises required direct contact and interaction with the Romans. Doing business with their unclean masters altered their purity status, affecting their state of holiness. One of the "most" unholy and defiling occupations was the collection of taxes. Somewhere in his life, Zacchaeus chose to work for Rome. He became a tax collector, and then a chief tax collector.

Some Background Regarding Rome's Tax System

Rome's taxation was highly organized, supported by their military, and was terribly harsh. After all, Rome had a vast empire to manage, and life in the capital was truly expensive. Caesar and the senate acquired their needed revenue from the vassal provinces.

> In the eyes of Rome the provinces were to carry the heavy weight of administering the Empire. Judea was in the province of Syria and every man was to pay 1% of his annual income for income tax. But that was not all, there were also import and export taxes, crop taxes (1/10 of grain crop and 1/5 of wine, fruit, and olive oil), sales tax, property tax, emergency tax, and on and on.
>
> Most of the time when the Bible mentions a publican, or a tax collector it is referring to a regular tax collector (publicanus) rather than a chief tax collector. The tax collectors were usually Jewish and therefore they were hated by their own people. When they collected their taxes for Rome they would turn over the required amount of money, and whatever they could add on for themselves is what they kept. They were known to be extortioners of large sums of money. Due to their relationship with Rome, the tax collectors were considered as Gentiles in the eyes of the Jews, and hated for their domination, they were treated similar to the worst kinds of sinners and prostitutes.[4]

The Spiritual Climate in First-Century Palestine

The religious atmosphere was supercharged by the various sects: the Pharisees and Sadducees, the Sanhedrin, the priesthood, and the elders, rabbis, and the Torah teachers. Their disagreements on the meaning of the law, the diversity and division between the north and south, and all the traditions and regional practices were overwhelming and impossible to keep up with and obey. There were mountains of judgment heaped on the backs of people for not measuring up. The leaders fought and argued with one another. In first-century Palestine, disobedience to the law and failing to live/keep the traditions were met with swift punishment. In many ways, the little guy didn't stand a chance.

What would have been the collective attitude of the Jews and that of their religious leaders toward a Jewish tax collector, a chief tax collector?

From the Greek Text

We return to our story. Zacchaeus didn't hold the respect of the Jewish people. Truth is, they hated him. The text says he was rich. Scripture doesn't qualify what that means, but it's safe to say that his fellow Jews were not rich. They would not only resent Zacchaeus for prospering at their expense but would resent him horribly for helping their oppressors sustain their tyranny. Perhaps the biggest issue with Zacchaeus was that he violated the holiness and purity laws. The monies and coinage collected had Caesar's inscription. That constituted graven images. If they were handled or touched, it left the holder defiled. Zacchaeus chose that life, and it was a life of separation. There was no sacrifice for him at the temple, no prayers at the local synagogue. He would not be welcome anywhere by anyone who was attempting to live up to the law. That was a lifetime of being unclean due to the choice he made. He was an anathema to his own people.

The text doesn't say why Zacchaeus went out to see Jesus. Was he curious? Was there a buzz moving through Jericho that something was happening? Did someone mention something about Jesus of Nazareth coming through town? Was he tired of being unclean? Did he yearn to return to spiritual and social life among his people? Whatever his reasons, Zacchaeus went out to see Jesus, and it's reasonable that he could have heard about him. Would there be some value to Zacchaeus just to see Jesus? Did he have any expectation of meeting him?

But as he went out to the road, there was already a crowd who would think him a sinner. All have sinned, and all are sinners, but in this context, the word meant something more. This was a reference to defilement, an accusation requiring them to separate from him, lest they defile themselves by accidental contact. Having seen him coming, would they turn their backs? Would anyone be willing to stand next to him? Would they keep their distance, not only for purity reasons but also due to the disdain they had for him?

The text says that Jesus was passing through, that he and his disciples were going up to Jerusalem. The text also says that Jesus saw Zacchaeus on the tree and did what the Messiah, the Shepherd, was prophesied to do. He reached out to a lost sheep of Israel. Zacchaeus was a son of Abraham. He was lost, separated from the flock of God. But he clearly longed to return. So Jesus said, "Come down, Zacchaeus. Immediately, I must stay at your house today!"

I can't imagine what this meant for Zacchaeus. Did he wonder if he heard Jesus right? Did he say, "Really, are you talking to me? You want to come home with me? You are willing to speak to me and associate with me and come into my house?" This was exceptional, incredible, and unheard of! Imagine Zacchaeus in that moment. What did this mean to him? How did it affect him? Was he already on his way to changing his life? When Zacchaeus offered to pay back four times the money, was he already striving to honor the spirit of the law? For what did Moses say about a fellow countryman who is struggling? Zacchaeus was complying with the law and even exceeding its demands.

> If your countrymen becomes poor and is unable to support himself among you, help him as you would an alien or a temporary resident, so he can continue to live among you. Do not take interest of any kind from him, but fear your God, so that your countryman may continue to live among you. (Leviticus 25:35–36)

> And if I say to the wicked man, "You will surely die," but then he turns away from his sin and does what is just and right, if he gives back what he took in pledge for a loan, returns what he has stolen, follows the decrees that give life, and does no evil, he will surely live; he will not die. None of the sins he has committed will be remembered against him. He has done what is just and right; he will surely live. (Ezekiel 33:14–16)

Jesus said to him, "Today salvation has come to this house because this man, too, is a son of Abraham." The Messiah offered Zacchaeus his moment, a chance for redemption and an opportunity to return to the flock of God. In every way, Zacchaeus stepped up and swung for the fence. He humbled himself, demonstrating to Jesus and the crowd his broken and contrite heart.

Zacchaeus climbed up a tree as an unclean, defiled sinner. When he came down, he was a changed man—cleansed, forgiven, and filled with the joy of salvation. Zacchaeus had returned to the flock of God.

You too are a son of Abraham. Welcome back, welcome home!

For Us Today

Great stories of great people inspire us all. When those stories are about second chances and the new beginnings of people redeemed in Jesus, well, it makes me appreciate Zacchaeus and his kind all the more.

Getting invited to dinner at their home was a great honor for us. The honor increased with the knowledge that we would be eating his famous five-alarm Texas chili. This was such a cool thing and would be the only cool thing about it! His chili was blazing hot. Getting together with them remains one of our fondest memories.

We knew them because Danielle had graduated from Lubbock Christian University and was headed to graduate school at Texas Tech. She needed to work for a while before starting her master's program and found a position with the Sunset Church of Christ there in Lubbock. She handled various assignments and administrative duties for some of the ministers; one of them, along with his wife, were our hosts that night.

On arriving, we were immediately led into the kitchen. A giant pot sat steaming on the stove, vapors rising from the peppers and chilies, filling the house with an incredible aroma. We sat at the kitchen table, and then he led us in prayer, and it was time to eat. There were Texas-sized bowls and spoons and mason jars for the iced tea. There was a lot of iced tea. Have I mentioned that the chili was hot? It was the kind of hot that people who know hot food think of as hot. From the moment it touched our tongues, it was hot. All the way down it was hot. This stuff could have removed wallpaper, just dissolve it off the wall. We each managed to finish our bowl, but just barely, and there wouldn't be seconds. Danielle did better than me since she possesses a world-class tolerance. Our host so enjoyed watching me suffer. Oh, he pretended to be concerned, but he actually just laughed all through dinner at my pain and suffering. It was so great.

It just blessed and enriched us to be in their home. They had such sweet affection for each other and acted like newlyweds. After dinner, we got to sit and talk, to hear his stories, and to ask the questions we longed to ask. As we drove home, we marveled at the amazing evening we had shared. It was a once-in-a-lifetime kind of thing for us. Part of what we marveled at was that a prison director had once referred to our host as "the meanest man in Texas." Our hosts for the evening were Clyde and Julia Thompson.

In 1928, Clyde confessed to shooting and killing two men. He and a couple of friends were hunting, using some guns belonging to the dad of one of his buddies. While hunting, they came upon two young men. One of the men held a grudge against the family of one of Clyde's friends. An argument started, erupting into a fight, and ended with the two young men being shot. Clyde was seventeen years old.

Clyde would be the youngest man in Texas to receive the death penalty. There would be appeals, hearings, and more trials, but to no avail. In 1931, Clyde was sent to death row at the Walls Unit in Huntsville, Texas. He was scheduled to be the eighty-third inmate executed in the electric chair. However, seven hours before his execution, Governor Ross Sterling stayed the execution and commuted his sentence to life in prison.

Clyde would ultimately be responsible for the deaths of eight men: the two he killed that sent him to prison and six more while inside prison. He would avoid the death penalty, and there were explanations for that, but he believed it was due to a higher purpose.

Early in his death-row experience, a guard played a radio throughout the day. Clyde could listen to it from his cell. Some of what he heard was from a broadcast by Brother Wilmeth, a Gospel preacher on the radio. In time, Clyde was able to ask him to come to the prison for a visit, and he agreed. As a result, Brother Wilmeth was able to baptize Clyde into Jesus. Soon he was taken off death row and was striving to live for God.

Not long after his baptism, he was transferred to the Retrieve Farm near Angleton, Texas. This was a bad place. They worked the inmates from daylight to dark, seven days a week, and for weeks at a time. During his time there, Clyde lost his new faith. On two different occasions, he engaged in knife fights, resulting in the deaths of two men. Clyde was relocated again to a special unit north of Huntsville dubbed Little Alcatraz. Although he made some escape attempts, each one failed.

The prison officials gave up. So they crafted a special cell for Clyde, converting an abandoned morgue that sat behind the death-row building. The morgue had six slabs to support six coffins. They put on a steel door that had a small bar-covered window; this was the only opening to the outside. His new cell was between two larger buildings, so Clyde only got sunlight through the window for five hours a day. At night, he lived in pitch-dark, having no electricity. They gave him shorts to wear, fearing that he might use the pants to hang himself. He ate with his fingers. He wasn't allowed eating utensils due to concern of his sharpening them to use against the guards. He had no bathroom facilities, just a bucket. He got a bath once a week. It was just an old abandoned morgue, and he would stay there for just over five years.

His saving grace came from his request for a Bible. He had lost his faith and no longer believed. But he knew they wouldn't allow him anything else to read. The Bible request was about boredom. Reading it would be something to do, something to engage his brain. Miracle of miracles, they gave him a New Testament. Clyde began to read. Quoting from Mr. Thompson,

> The more I studied it, the more it convinced me that it was a book of truth and I was false. When I came to realize that this was actually the word of God and the only hope for man in this world, I repented in tears, on my knees day and night for months. I read the Bible and kept asking God if He could and would forgive a wretch like me, and take me and use me to His honor and glory. He did. I began to write articles for Christian papers, some of you may remember reading them many years ago. Christian friends would write me and send me literature, and I would take that literature and hand it to other people.

In time, Clyde was transferred out of the morgue. They placed him in Ramsey Farm, and he did well there. He helped to put on Christmas plays using the inmates. By the time he left Ramsey Farm, he was teaching a Bible class with eighty-one inmates, sixty of whom had been baptized. Eventually he came up for parole, but the board decided to put it off for another three years.

He became acquainted with a Christian lady through a mutual acquaintance, a preacher friend. The two began exchanging letters. She visited him, and in time, they fell in love. They dreamed of being married, but everyone said it was hopeless. Clyde Thompson, people said, was never going to walk out of prison. She worked tirelessly for his release. For five years, she worked to free him. The prayers and efforts paid off, to the surprise and astonishment of just about everyone! After twenty-eight years and two months, Clyde Thompson walked out of prison. Julia was there to meet him, with a new suit, a borrowed shirt, and a tie. Clyde had never owned a suit, had never worn a tie. Clyde and Julia got married.

They devoted the next twenty years of their lives to helping prisoners, teaching them the grace of God and spreading the Gospel. They helped those newly released from prison. Clyde invited them home. He gave them a suit of clothes and engaged them in conversation about Jesus. I wonder if he served them chili?

Clyde Thomson served on the staff for the Sunset church. He ministered to those in the county jail and did whatever he could to help inmates know Jesus. We knew Clyde because Danielle worked for him. One amazing night, we were invited to dinner. To us, he was bigger than life and had the personality to match. Clyde passed away of a heart attack July 1, 1979, just a few months after our dinner.

I'm not suggesting that Clyde and Zacchaeus were the same—they weren't—except to say that both were sinners and both were in desperate need of salvation. Jesus offered acceptance, fellowship, and salvation to the hated tax collector, and he offered it to the meanest man in Texas prisons. Each was loved, and each was forgiven. Grace and mercy. Salvation and redemption. Pardon and forgiveness. Jesus came to seek and to save the lost. He came for Zacchaeus and for Clyde. And he came for us.

From the law and the prophets, I realize how important holiness is to God. He has always desired a people who would live for His honor. From the Messiah, I realize how important it is to God to share His holiness with us. Jesus, the Messiah—he was there for the tree climber, the chili maker, and for you and me.

> I thank Christ Jesus our Lord, who has given me strength, that he considered me faithful, appointing me to his service. Even though I was once a blasphemer and a persecutor and a violent man, I was shown mercy because I acted in ignorance and unbelief. The grace of our Lord was poured out on me abundantly, along with the faith and love that are in Christ Jesus. Here is a trustworthy saying that deserves full acceptance; Christ Jesus came into the world to save sinners, of whom I am the worst.
>
> —1 Timothy 1:12–15

10

Saying No to the Greatest Ever

Herod the Great was the ruthless king of Judea. He possessed a ravenous ambition for power, was highly skilled politically, and was morally deficient. He had an unfathomable appetite for building things—great things, lasting structures devoted mostly to his own glory. Some of his more well-known projects were Caesarea Maritima, the Herodium, Masada, his Jerusalem Palace, the Tomb of the Patriarchs, and of course, the great Temple Mount.[1] Herod proved quite cunning at currying favor with Rome, with Caesar and the Senate. He was king of Judea but really served Rome and her emperors.[2]

Never one to tolerate threats to his crown, Herod quickly and violently eliminated those who came between him and his power. This proved true even among his own family. Herod had ten wives and many children. He executed one of his wives and three of his sons, as well as other members of his family. When he heard about the newborn king of the Jews, he wasted no time in crafting a plot to have Jesus murdered. But of course, he failed. Joseph and Mary took Jesus and fled to Egypt, escaping Herod's plot.

After a few years, Herod died; and his son Archelaus came to power, but he didn't last long. His next son Antipas took the crown to reign over Judea. It was Herod Antipas who would have significant impact on both Jesus and John the Baptist.

Herod Antipas and John the Baptist

Herod Antipas proved just as proficient as his father in eliminating his enemies. And why shouldn't he? He learned it from the best. Although John the Baptist wasn't a rival to Antipas's throne, he did become a threat. In a strange turn of events, Antipas had John beheaded not because John threatened his throne but because he was an outspoken opponent of his sin.

The story unfolds in Matthew 14:1–12. Herod Antipas had developed a liking for Herodias, his brother Philip's wife. She didn't seem to mind the king's attention. John spoke out boldly against Antipas, saying that he had no right to take Herodias for himself, that it was unlawful for him to have his brother's wife. Well, this wouldn't do if you were the king and were bent on having what you wanted. So Herod ordered John arrested and imprisoned. Antipas wanted to kill John, but he was afraid of the people because they considered John a prophet. And rightly so, for Jesus said of John,

> Then what did you go out to see? A prophet? Yes, I tell you, and more than a prophet. This is the one about whom it is written: I will send my messenger ahead of you, who will prepare your way before you. I tell you the truth: Among those born of women there has not risen anyone greater than John the Baptist; yet he who is least in the kingdom of heaven is greater than he. (Matthew 11:9–11)

It wouldn't be popular to execute a prophet of God. Since Herod Antipas had to rule over the people, he was content to let John sit in prison. However, on Herod's birthday, Salome, Herodias's daughter, danced for the king. It must have been some dance! When she finished, Herod was moved to promise her anything her heart desired. She consulted with her mother, who told her to ask for John's death, happily thinking this would end John's condemnation of them. So the dancing daughter asked for John's head on a platter. This put Antipas in a tight spot. On the one hand, he didn't want to upset the Jews by killing John; but on the other hand, he had promised the girl in front of his guests. You don't want to disappoint your party guests. Most people just have cake and ice cream, and maybe some balloons, but not Herod. Does it seem especially wicked, blatantly evil, that John was killed because Antipas couldn't control his craven appetites? Jesus referred to John as the greatest man ever born. And the greatest of us all ended up beheaded as entertainment at a birthday party.

John and the Christ

Prior to Herod's party, and already in prison, John heard about what the Christ was doing in his ministry. Given the context of Matthew 11, what John would have heard about were the miracles Jesus performed, the people he was healing, and the good news of the kingdom he was preaching in the towns of Galilee. The text records that John sent some disciples with instructions to ask Jesus this rather curious question: "Are you the one who was to come, or should we expect someone else?" (John 11:3).

Please note the wording of the text: "When John heard in prison what the Christ was doing." It doesn't say "when John heard what *Jesus* was doing" or "when John heard what the *Rabbi* was doing" but "what the *Christ* was doing." Is this significant to the story? Matthew used the word *Christ* four times in chapter 1, once in chapter 2, and then not again until this text. By referring to "Christ," Matthew alerts the reader that what follows relates to the Messiah being the anointed of God, and to the prophecies about the anointed one's identity.

This was a really interesting question considering John and Jesus's history. First of all, we know the two were related. Their mothers, Mary and Elizabeth, were relatives (Luke 1:34–37). Although there's not a text clarifying the nature of their relationship, it would still be likely that John and Jesus knew each other. The text reveals that, at some point, probably early in his life, John went out to live in the desert (Luke 1:80). We don't know his age when this happened.

When Jesus was ready to launch his ministry, he found John at the Jordan River and asked John to immerse him (Matthew 3:13–14). John recognized Jesus and apparently knew him, saying to him, "I need to be baptized by you, and do you come to me?" John's baptism was about spiritual renewal and preparation. John came to prepare the people for Messiah, whose coming was at hand. He prepared them by preaching a message of repentance, encouraging the Jewish people to turn their hearts to God and to their families (Luke 1:17). This was spiritual transformation, changing their hearts and minds, assuring they were spiritually and symbolically pure and ready for Messiah.[3]

Clearly, John had some understanding and awareness of Jesus. He humbled himself to Jesus, a rabbi and his relative.[4] At the very least, John recognized Jesus as someone spiritually superior to himself. Consider John 1:29–34:

> The next day John saw Jesus coming toward him and said, "Look, the Lamb of God, who takes away the sin of the world. This is the one I meant when I said, 'A man who comes after me has surpassed me because he was before me.' I myself did not know him, but the reason I came baptizing with water was that he might be revealed to Israel."

Then John gave this testimony:

> I saw the Spirit come down from heaven as a dove and
> remain on him. I would not have known him, except
> that the one who sent me to baptize with water told
> me, "The man on whom you see the Spirit come down
> and remain is he who will baptize with the Holy
> Spirit." I have seen and I testify that this is the Son
> of God.

John said that he would not have known Jesus if the
Lord hadn't revealed it to him. It's hard to accept the notion
that John had never met Jesus, or that he didn't know him,
or that he didn't know they were related. Instead, I take
this to mean that John didn't fully realize that Jesus was the
Messiah. This better fits the text. John knew his mission was
to reveal the Anointed One to Israel. But did he fully grasp
that his relative, Jesus from Nazareth, was the Messiah?
Perhaps not. The voice of God at Jesus's baptism was as
much for John's benefit as it was for Jesus or anyone else.
"This is my Son, whom I love; with him I am well pleased"
(Matthew 3:17). "I would not have known him" was John
revealing that he didn't know Jesus as the Messiah.

Back to Matthew 11 and the Question

John knew that Jesus was the Messiah, so what was
behind his question, "Are you the one who was to come,
or should we expect someone else?" Was he having doubts,
questioning if Jesus really was the Christ? Or was John's
question about something else? Notice the beginning part
of the text: "When John heard...what Christ *was doing*."

What was it that Jesus was "doing"? Whatever it was,
it decidedly shaped John's question. Either John heard
something that caused him to doubt, or he heard something

that triggered his question for a different reason. The purpose of the question is perhaps made clear if we can identify whatever it was that John heard Jesus was doing.

What Was Jesus Doing?

My earlier understanding of this text had me thinking that John was questioning Jesus's ministry, believing that Jesus wasn't acting Messiah-like. The earlier position held that John expected Jesus to be busy restoring the kingdom (i.e., rallying the troops, pushing against Rome, reestablishing David's throne). My thinking was that John, like Jesus's disciples, was looking for Jesus to restore a national kingdom. So in John's eyes, when he heard about what Jesus was doing, or what he wasn't doing, he began to doubt. Jesus wasn't preaching a message of nationalism or a physical restoration of Israel, so I concluded that John doubted Jesus for these reasons. But I was wrong. My position was formulated based on not knowing the prophecies about Messiah or realizing that John was a rabbi with the Holy Spirit and possessed a clear and sound understanding.

So I've had to reject that earlier interpretation. What John heard about what Jesus was doing was all plainly rooted in messianic prophecy. Jesus's message and ministry emanated from the Torah, the psalms, and the prophets. John was a prophet himself, and the people called him *rabbi* (Matthew 11:9, 14:5, 21:46; John 3:26). As a prophet and rabbi, John would have the scriptures memorized. He possessed a full working knowledge of Torah. He knew what the Messiah was prophesied to teach and what his ministry was to do.

From the Hebrew Text

To better understand, we must go back to the roots and examine what the prophets predicted the Anointed One would do to serve the people. Let's see if Jesus was in fact carrying out the prophetic vision of the Messiah. When the Messiah comes, he would do the following:

1. Heal the blind
   - Psalm 146:8
   - Isaiah 29:18
   - Isaiah 35:5
   - Isaiah 42:7
   - Isaiah 43:7–9

2. Heal the lame
   - Isaiah 35:6
   - Jeremiah 31:8
   - Micah 4:6–7
   - Zephaniah 3:19

3. Heal the diseased
   - Isaiah 53:4 (infirmities)
   - 2 Kings 5 (only God can heal leprosy, Jesus healed lepers, Jesus is God)

4. Heal the deaf
   - Isaiah 29:18
   - Isaiah 35:5
   - Isaiah 43:7–9

5. Raise the dead
   - Isaiah 26:19
6. Preach good news to the poor
   - Isaiah 52:7
   - Isaiah 61:1
7. Release the captives
   - Isaiah 49:9
   - Isaiah 61:1
   - Zechariah 9:11

The prophets preached a message of messianic hope. They preached to those in need of a brighter future and to those in need of repentance. Their preaching spoke of a shepherd, one who would bind their wounds. He would be a true shepherd who would seek the brokenhearted and restore them to the flock.

From the Greek Text

And so what was Jesus doing? What were the "things" John heard about? The answer to this question is provided in Matthew chapters 9 and 10. These texts give a detailed picture of "the things" John heard about. What these chapters reveal about Jesus is that he was busy helping people. He was ministering to the lost sheep of Israel, healing, restoring people to God, and teaching and preaching a message of hope to the masses. Consider this brief overview of Matthew 9 and 10.

From Chapter 9

Jesus could be found doing the following in this chapter:

1. He healed a paralyzed man (vv. 1–8).

2. He forgave a paralyzed man's sins (vv. 1–8).

3. He called Matthew, a tax collector, to become a disciple (vv. 9–13).

4. He entered Matthew's house and had table fellowship with him and his sinful friends (vv. 9–13).

5. He was questioned why he allowed his followers to break tradition (vv. 14–17).

6. He healed a sick woman (vv. 20–22).

7. He raised a girl back to life (vv. 23–26).

8. He healed two blind men (vv. 27–31).

9. He healed a deaf man (vv. 32–34.

This chapter has Jesus healing, resurrecting, forgiving, and calling men to discipleship.

From Chapter 10

This whole chapter is devoted to Jesus showing his disciples how to preach and how to serve others. Then Jesus sent them out to preach and to heal in the same manner he had demonstrated for them.

Take careful note of the things Jesus did in chapters 9 and 10: He healed the blind, the lame, the diseased, and the deaf. He raised the dead. He preached the good news of the kingdom. He forgave sins and sent his disciples to preach and minister to the people. Many of these people were considered to be unrepentant sinners and, therefore, were unclean and defiled. As such, they were judged and considered anathema. They were sheep that were lost and unwanted—except by Jesus, who loved and wanted every one of them. Now take a look at what Jesus said to the messengers in response to John's question.

> Jesus replied, "Go back and report to John what you hear and see: The blind receive sight, the lame walk, those who have leprosy [skin diseases] are cured, the deaf hear, the dead are raised, and the good news is preached to the poor." (Matthew 11:4–5)

Jesus sent them back to John to deliver this message, that Jesus was daily serving the people of Israel by healing, helping, forgiving, and offering them the good news. He wanted John to know that he was doing the following:

1. Healing the blind
2. Healing the lame
3. Curing lepers
4. Healing the deaf
5. Raising the dead
6. Preaching good news to the poor

These are precisely the miracles and ministry that Jesus demonstrated in Matthew 9 and 10. So what effect does this have on John's question? Jesus was doing everything the Prophets prophesied the Messiah would do, except for one thing. There was an additional service Jesus left off his list. Did he fail to mention it? Was it a momentary lapse? Does that sound like Jesus?

Jesus told John's messengers, "Go back and report to John what you hear and see."

- The blind receive sight.
- The lame walk.
- Those who have leprosy (skin diseases) are cured.
- The deaf hear.
- The dead are raised.
- Good news is preached to the poor.

What Jesus didn't mention was that the Messiah was also to "proclaim freedom for the captives and release for the prisoners." This was a common and enthusiastic prophecy regarding the Messiah.

> Say to the captives, "Come out" and to those in darkness, "Be free." (Isaiah 49:9)
>
> To proclaim freedom for the captives and release for the prisoners. (Isaiah 61:1)

But Jesus doesn't mention the prisoners or the captives in his message to John. It wasn't a mistake but an intentional omission. There are many interpretations of Matthew 11, but I have embraced the idea that what John was really asking, in his Jewish and rabbinical manner, was this: "Jesus, are you going to set me free, are you going to release me from prison?"

The answer Jesus sent back to John was in response to what John heard about Jesus. John knew these messianic texts, which spoke of healings, resurrections, freedom, and good news. He was counting on them. Was John asking about his own freedom? Was he one of the prisoners he hoped the Messiah would set free?

In every way, Jesus was carrying out the prophetic ministry revealed in the Old Testament. Well, almost in every way. By leaving off the "release of captives," Jesus was communicating to John that he would remain in prison. It's as if Jesus was telling him, "I'm saying yes to the blind, deaf, and lame. I'm saying yes to the lepers and even to the dead. But, John, I'm saying no to releasing the captives, at least in your situation." Jesus knew the messengers would go back and tell John what Jesus had said. And he knew John would understand. This was Jesus saying no to the greatest ever.

It's a really hard thing, and sad. John would remain where he was, and his life would end in prison. He would be beheaded and put on display for the amusement of Herod's guests. His death would serve no better purpose than entertainment and to put an end to John's condemnation of Herod and Herodias. Or was there an even greater purpose? For didn't John say, "He must become greater, and I must become less." Sometimes we grasp the purpose of God but have no idea how He will carry out His purpose in our lives. It can be hard to understand and even harder to accept.

Does John's story in any way challenge your understanding of Jesus? Does it bother you that he allowed John to die? It causes me to reflect on the last piece of Jesus's message back to John, which was, "Blessed is the man who does not fall away on account of me."

Here is Jesus boldly stating that of those born of women, John is the greatest. Yet he is willing for John to remain in prison and to suffer a violent death. This is Jesus saying no. Has he said no before? Have others asked for his help, and he refused them?

Remember John 11, when his friends asked him to heal their brother, Lazarus? They said to him, "Lord, the one you love is sick" (see John 11:3). But Jesus didn't go to Bethany; instead he stayed where he was for a few more days. Meanwhile, Lazarus died and was buried. Then Jesus took his disciples and went to Bethany. The sisters were filled with grief, confusion, and perhaps even anger. They wept and Jesus wept with them. He wept even though he could have prevented his friend's death. But that's not the end of the story.

Jesus called for Lazarus to come out of the tomb, and to his family's delight and the crowd's amazement, he did. But giving Lazarus back to the sisters wasn't the only result. Remember, it was prophesied that the Messiah would raise the dead, a sign of the Messiah. Due to Lazarus's resurrection, many more Jews believed in Jesus (John 11:45). The growing belief among the Jews because of Lazarus stirred up even more animosity toward Jesus, and his enemies plotted to kill him (John 11:46–50, 53).

Think about it. If Jesus had healed Lazarus when he received the news of his illness, would even more of the Jews have come to faith? The resurrection was the catalyst for their belief. And if many people hadn't believed, would there have been the rise in animosity and subsequent plan to kill him? In John 12:17–18, the crowd was continuing to spread the news about Lazarus's resurrection, and many people wanted to see Jesus and get to know him. The enemies of Christ were growing more desperate by the hour (v. 19). Jesus was crucified because angry people begged for it to happen. Much of their anger was due to his followers growing in number, to the crowd's growing interest, and the revival his ministry created. If Jesus had simply healed Lazarus, would all of that have happened? When his hour had come, they killed him. Salvation depended on his resurrection. His resurrection depended on his death, which depended on his crucifixion.

Jesus said no to some of his closest, most beloved friends. It's hard to see him say no to friends—to John , Lazarus, to Mary, and Martha—and, at times, to his closest disciples.

For Us Today

Is it true that God will allow me to hurt, suffer, and experience grief if it benefits his kingdom? Does he allow these things to happen if, in doing so, it advances His divine plans? Does this divine dynamic carry out even if I don't understand how my pain serves His purpose? Is this not what the Father did with His own Son?

And how about us? How do we feel about Jesus saying no when we find ourselves needing him? Isn't he the Good Shepherd? Isn't he the one who leaves the flock to search for and find the one hurting lamb? I confess there have been moments when I have said what Martha said, "Lord, if you had been here, my brother would not have died."

One afternoon in May of 1983, my wife, Danielle, went into labor, our first. The pain was mild—it was early—but soon things began to develop. That evening, the NBA playoffs were on, and the team we loved to watch was doing well against the team we loved to hate. But things progressed, and it was time to get to the hospital. We arrived and the hospital folks did as they do; and in no time, we were in the delivery room, hooked up to monitors, and gearing up for the happiest moment of our lives. She continued to dilate, and everything was progressing well.

Then one of the nurses, while checking the fetal monitor, noticed something that, at the moment, slipped by us. But she would keep checking. Then she brought in another nurse to check the monitor. Together they decided the lead wasn't working properly. Our family doctor came in right as the nurses were struggling with the lead wire that attached to the monitor. He quickly examined the situation and determined the lead was not on the baby at all. He promptly removed the lead, inserted and connected a new one, and that's when things rapidly went from concerning to frightening.

Having attached the new lead, it was obvious that our baby's heart wasn't beating, or wasn't beating normally. Our OB arrived and immediately called for Danielle to be taken to the OR. She would have an emergency C-section, the decision being that our baby was in distress and needed to get out as quickly as possible. Since this was emergency surgery, I wasn't allowed inside, so I paced the hallway for about thirty minutes, but it seemed so much longer.

Finally our family doctor and the OB came out to speak with me. As best they could, they explained that our baby had already died prior to the surgery. There was nothing they could have done. In fact, it was determined that he had died sometime earlier that evening. It was a premature separation of the upper placenta, they would later tell us. The nurse had attached the fetal-monitor lead onto Danielle's cervix by mistake; the heartbeat that was registering on the screen was hers, not the baby's. Due to her heartbeat being slower than what the baby's should have been, they began thinking something was wrong with the lead. Once a new lead was fixed on the baby, there wasn't a heartbeat to register.

I got in to recovery to see Danielle as quickly as they would allow. She was groggy but awake, and they had already explained to her what happened. It was one-thirty in the morning. She was drifting in and out of sleep, still struggling with the anesthesia. A nurse came in and asked if I wanted to see the baby, to hold him. At that moment, I was somewhere in between numbness and pain and wasn't prepared for the question. Danielle was asleep at that moment, so I gathered myself, said yes, and walked with her down to the delivery room.

They had him cleaned up and wrapped in a blue blanket with a little cap on his head. The nurse picked him up and asked if I wanted to hold him. I wasn't sure if I did, wasn't sure if I didn't and wasn't sure if I could. She just placed him in my arms. I held him for several minutes, counted his fingers and toes. It seemed like he was just asleep. Eventually I asked if it was all right to take him back to our room. I knew Danielle would want to see him, to hold him. So I gently woke her and placed our son, Jared Richard, in her arms. There we were, the three of us, in the middle of the night, hurting and crying and feeling like our world had collapsed. We were a family, if only for a few minutes. I said a prayer. We said good-bye. And the nurse took him away.

Later, as the sun began to rise, I found myself asking God why He said no. For the half hour that Danielle was in surgery, I was praying, and praying hard. I asked, begged, and bargained. I pleaded. The doctor had prepped me for the possibility that this wasn't going to turn out well. But still I prayed. And he still died. On a long and horrible night in May of 1983, God said no to me. He had the power. He could have prevented it, kept it from happening. But He didn't. Why? What purpose did this serve? Like Martha, I kept thinking, *Jesus, if you had only been here, my son would not have died.*

Through the years, we have stood at the bedside of other young mothers who lost their babies. We have embraced their young husbands. I have hugged and comforted those who were facing exactly what I faced. I have presided at the funerals for babies who died soon after their birth, for babies who died in accidents, for children who died entirely too early in life. I can't say that we lost our baby so we could know how to comfort others, but we have. Did losing our son have some greater purpose in God's kingdom? Maybe. Will we ever know? Was God being cruel by causing our baby to die? I don't believe so. But I do believe that He, in His universal wisdom, used our grief and pain as a catalyst to produce faith and courage in our hearts and in the hearts of others; for certainly, such courage was going to be needed as we moved forward with our lives. If Jesus said no to the greatest ever, might he also say no to me?

I can't say what purpose John's dying served. Did he know? With Mary, Martha, and Lazarus, it's transparent— at least it is for us because we see the whole story. But so much of the time, we are faced with gut-wrenching heartache and struggle with asking why. Why didn't He intervene? Why is he allowing me to go through this? I don't understand. Why does God say no to me?

John asked, "Lord, are you the one who is to come?" Jesus could only encourage John to not give up, to not fall away on account of him. Don't give up, John. Don't quit. I know you are hurting, confused, and in doubt, but there is blessing in keeping your heart rooted in God. There is reward in not falling away. Keep on going and keep believing that, in the end, all will be made right. God will be the answer to all your questions. He is at the end of all things, and the end will be awesome!

> Be joyful always, pray continually; give thanks in all circumstances, for this is God's will for you in Christ Jesus.
>
> —1 Thessalonians 5:16–18

Part III

How Messiah's Death Completed God's Purpose

11

A Tale of Two Gardens

Growing and maintaining a beautiful garden has always mystified me. Those I've attempted to grow have resulted in a mixed bag of success and failure. At times, the plants and flowers flourish, at least for a while. But soon, and inevitably, either the unwanted grasses sprout up or the unwelcome weeds take over. In my consternation, I begin to ignore the daily tasks of good gardening. Soon the lovely colors begin to fade, replaced by every thriving and unwanted thing, which grow tall, strong, and healthy, and without any help from me. Beautiful, well-kept gardens require gardeners with passion, skills, and commitment, of which I have none. Oh well, at least I can appreciate the gardens of others, especially some of that are mentioned in scripture.

The Bible mentions a number of gardens, and this chapter will focus on two of them. They are known as the Garden of Eden and the garden of Gethsemane. Together, they represent *a tale of two gardens.*

The first one is known for being where Adam and Eve committed the sin that resulted in death. The second one is famous for being where Jesus submitted to death, that resulted in life. It could be said that every important thing that's happened to mankind happened in these two gardens.

Eden was where sin emerged, innocence was lost, and open fellowship with God came to a disappointing end.

Gethsemane was where Jesus prayed about the salvation of the world and his role in achieving that salvation. Actually, he prayed three times, making the same request with each prayer—that his Father would find another way. It was in Gethsemane that Jesus submitted to his Father's will. His submission meant surrendering to those who craved his crucifixion. They unknowingly crucified the Anointed One. The Tale of Two Gardens: the first was where man became lost through sin, and the second was where man was saved by the forgiveness of sin. Let's take a closer look at both of these gardens.

From the Hebrew Text

First, let's go back to the Garden of Eden and review what happened. Perhaps Eden's garden will lead us to Gethsemane, and Gethsemane will lead us to Jesus our Messiah.

The Garden Paradise

God created Eden specifically for Adam and placed him there, alone. Adam hadn't been wandering around and then one day stumbled into Eden. He didn't accidently discover it. This was the place God prepared for him.

> Now The Lord God had planted a garden in the east, in Eden; and there he put the man he had formed... The Lord God took the man and put him in the Garden of Eden to work it and take care of it. And the Lord God commanded the man, "You are free to eat from any tree in the garden; but you must not eat from the tree of the knowledge of good and evil, for when you eat of it you will surely die." (Genesis 2:8, 15–17)

Adam was in the garden, but he was alone. Yes, he walked with God; but God created Adam biologically, emotionally, and physically to need a mate, to be loved, and to have someone to love.

> The Lord God said, 'It is not good for man to be alone. I will make a suitable helper for him.".... Then The Lord God made a woman from the rib he had taken out of the man, and he brought her to the man. The man said, "This is now bone of my bones and flesh of my flesh; she shall be called woman, for she was taken out of man." (Genesis 2: 18, 22)

When God saw what he had created, He pronounced it "very good." The good of God's creation encompassed all he had made, but in this context, it specifically emphasized Adam and Eve in the perfect Garden of Eden (Genesis 1:31).

There are many aspects about their garden experience for which few details are provided. There are some things I can't help wondering about:

- How big was the garden: an acre, a hundred acres?
- How many kinds of fruit trees did they have?
- Did they live in some kind of house?
- Did they get sick?
- Did they know fear?
- They were naked, so did they get cold? Did they have fire?
- Did they have any struggles at all?

We know that Eden was a beautiful and harmonious place. We might think, *Surely they had nothing to worry about. No actual problems, right?* What was it like to live in a perfect place?

Here is a list of some things they probably didn't have to contend with:

- Guilt
- Remorse
- Sadness
- Depression
- Anger
- Resentment
- Conflict
- Hatred
- Bitterness
- Stress
- Jealousy
- Fear
- Illness
- Death

It's interesting that *Eden* means "fruitful, or well-watered." The word can be translated as "pleasure, delight, or luxury."[1] Adam and Eve lived in a place with an abundance of clean water and with all the fresh fruit they could eat. It was a garden paradise—delightful and luxurious. They didn't have sin, so they didn't know shame. They were naked before God and each other. They were free, blessed, and had every need met. God provided for them. It was perfect.

Sin Enters the World

It is hard to imagine living without sin, without its brokenness and pain. So much of our struggle comes from existing in a fallen world, a world that was unknown to Adam and Eve. However, as beautiful as Eden was, it was still a place that offered a single temptation—evil had its presence.

> Now the serpent was more crafty than any of the wild animals the Lord God had made. He said to the woman, "Did God really say, 'You must not eat from any tree in the garden?'"
>
> When the woman saw that the fruit of the tree was good for food and pleasing to the eye, and also desirable for gaining wisdom, she took some and ate it. She also gave some to her husband, who was with her, and he ate it.
>
> Then the man and his wife heard the sound of The Lord God as he was walking in the garden in the cool of the day, and they hid from The Lord God among the trees of the garden. But The Lord God called to the man, "Where are you?" He answered, "I heard you in the garden, and I was afraid, because I was naked; so I hid." And he said, "Who told you that you were naked? Have you eaten from the tree that I commanded you not to eat from?" The man said, "The woman you put here with me, she gave me some fruit from the tree, and I ate it." Then The Lord God said to the woman, "What is this you have done?" The woman said, "The Serpent deceived me, and I ate." (Genesis 3:1, 6, 8–13)

Genesis 3 contains four distinct consequences to their actions:

1. The serpent was cursed, his head to be crushed (Genesis 3:14–15).

2. Women would have increased pain in childbirth (Genesis 3:16).

3. Adam was reduced to farming cursed ground (Genesis 3:17–19).

4. They were banished from the garden forever (Genesis 3:23).

Both Adam and Eve were held accountable for their actions. But after they sinned, God was specifically looking for Adam to speak to him. The covenant between them was that God would provide everything Adam needed, and Adam would honor God by keeping the one commandment. The first covenant between God and man was broken, and Adam did the breaking.

A Broken World

God's intent was to live in harmony with the only creation that shared His image. He placed within humanity a divine spark. In a sense, we share the same spiritual DNA.

Adam had one commandment—*one*! Under the Law of Moses, the people had 613 commandments. Adam had only one, and he couldn't keep it. Remember, Adam and Eve lived in a covenant that was based on law; it provided no grace. There was no second chance, no pardon, and no redemption. "For the day you eat of this tree you will surely die," God had said to them. Adam became the symbol for sinful mankind, carrying the stigma of shame (Romans 5:12–13).

One way or another, it was bound to happen, for all have sinned and fallen short of the glory of God (Romans 3:23). But let's not be too hard on him. To be honest, I think I would have caved even sooner than he did. Since Adam's fall, man has been "caving" and "crashing" by the billions. We live in a broken world, and each of us has contributed to its brokenness. It began in a garden with Adam's failure; a whole and perfect world was never going to last. Mankind created its own crisis; we were in conflict and needed help with our separation from God.

The Sin Solution

The solution, however, wasn't found in the goodness of man or in man's ability to regain his righteousness. No, like Adam, we just couldn't keep our hands off that fruit.

Neither was the solution found in the Law of Moses with its Aaronic priesthood and animal sacrifices. The sacrifices were only a reminder of sin and guilt and were unable to cleanse the conscience of the worshiper (Hebrews 9:9, 10:2–3). Yes, the law was perfect and good. It just required man's perfection, and man wasn't perfect.

No, the solution to our separation would not be found in the goodness of men or in the keeping of law. We needed a lasting sacrifice and a better covenant. We needed the Anointed of God, the descendant God promised to Abraham through the blood covenant, the one who would bless the nations. We needed Jesus. Lets look in on him as he prays in the garden of Gethsemane

From the Greek Text

The Garden of Gethsemane

Gethsemane has great historical and spiritual meaning for believers. The exact location in the garden where Jesus prayed is difficult to pinpoint. But its meaning cannot be diminished by not knowing the exact spot where he prayed.

Dr. William M. Thomson, author of *The Land and the Book*, first published in 1880, wrote:

> When I first came to Jerusalem, and for many years afterward, this plot of ground was open to all whenever they chose to come and meditate beneath its very old olive trees. The Latins, however, have within the last few years succeeded in gaining sole possession, and have built a high wall around it. The Greeks have invented another site a little to the north of it. My own impression is that both are wrong. The position is too near the city, and so close to what must have always been the great thoroughfare eastward, that our Lord would scarcely have selected it for retirement on that dangerous and dismal night. I am inclined to place the garden in the secluded vale several hundred yards to the north-east of the present Gethsemane.[2]

This from seetheholyland.net, "Gethsemane":[3]

> The garden, about 1200 square meters in area, was well known to the disciples as it was close to the natural route from the Temple to the summit of the Mount of Olives and the ridge leading to Bethany.

Jesus and his disciples were familiar with Gethsemane and the small villages in the area. On the evening of his arrest, he was there in the garden of Gethsemane, struggling with being God's anointed and asking his Father to remove the burden of the cross.

Jesus: In His Final Week

During Passover week, Jesus went each morning to the temple courts, to teach and to heal. In the evening, he and his disciples went to the Mount of Olives, where they most likely stayed with their friends Martha and Mary in Bethany or possibly with Simon the leper.

> Each day Jesus was teaching at the temple, and each evening he went out to spend the night on the hill called the Mount of Olives, and all the people came early in the morning to hear him at the temple. (Luke 21:37–38)

> But Jesus went to the Mount of Olives. At dawn he appeared again in the temple courts; where all the people gathered around him, and he sat down to teach them. (John 8:1–2)

During that week, Jesus was serving, teaching, and healing people. They witnessed him performing miracles and doing some amazing things. He cleansed the temple by driving out the money changers (Matthew 21:12–16). He gave the seven pronouncements against the Pharisees (Matthew 23:1–39) and taught his disciples the signs of the end-times. He was anointed while in Simon's house (Mark 14:1–9). He observed the widow giving her "two very small copper coins" (Luke 21:1–4). Toward the end of the week, he and his disciples shared their final meal together. Afterward, he took them up to the Mount of Olives and entered the garden of Gethsemane.

Richard N. Fyffe

Jesus in the Garden

> Then Jesus went with his disciples to a place called
> Gethsemane, and he said to them, "Sit here while I
> go over there and pray." He took Peter, and the two
> sons of Zebedee along with him, and he began to be
> sorrowful and troubled. Then he said to them, "My
> soul is overwhelmed with sorrow to the point of
> death. Stay here and keep watch with me." Going a
> little further, he fell down with his face to the ground
> and prayed, "My Father, if it is possible, may this cup
> be taken from me. Yet not as I will, but as you will."
> (Matthew 26:36–39)

Luke records this aspect of Jesus in the garden:

> An angel from heaven appeared to him and
> strengthened him. And being in anguish, he prayed
> more earnestly, and his sweat was like drops of blood
> falling to the ground. (Luke 22:43–44)

The text states the following:

1. Jesus was sorrowful and troubled, his soul overwhelmed to the point of death.
2. He was in anguish, and his sweat fell to the ground
   like drops of blood.

Do you see these words? Can you feel them? He was
sorrowful, troubled, and anguished. He was overwhelmed
to the point of death, and his sweat was falling like drops of
blood to the ground.

Jesus repeated his prayer about the cup two more times.
I have wondered why. Was Jesus waiting for an audible
answer from the Father? Did he need to hear Him say
either, "Yes, I will remove the cup" or "No, the cup will not

be taken away from you"? Did he not know the purpose for which he came to earth? There is plenty of textual evidence that Jesus knew exactly why he had come to earth. He told his disciples on numerous occasions that he would suffer, die on the cross, and be raised in three days. Jesus knew his purpose. So why was he asking?

I believe the garden of Gethsemane revealed Jesus in one of his most human moments, perhaps the most human of all. It's as if he was saying, "Please, Father, don't make me do this. Don't make me drink the bitter cup of suffering and shame." He asked three times, and it was the third time that his sweat began to fall like blood. There are various explanations for this bloodlike sweat. Here is one of them:

> [Hemidrosis or hematidrosis] results in the excretion of blood or blood pigment in the sweat. Under conditions of great emotional stress, tiny capillaries in the sweat glands can rupture, thus mixing blood with perspiration. This condition has been reported in extreme instances of stress...Acute fear and intense mental contemplation are found to be the most frequent inciting causes...While the extent of blood loss generally is minimal, hematidrosis also results in the skin becoming extremely tender and fragile, which would have made Christ's pending physical insults even more painful.[4]

This text is even more meaningful when we realize that it was cold the night Jesus was praying in the garden.

> It was cold, and the servants and officials stood around a fire they had made to keep warm. Peter also was standing with them, warming himself. (John 18:18)

Jesus was perspiring not because it was a warm and humid evening but because of the heavy stress and crushing pressure.

Jesus Under Extreme Pressure

Gethsemane was an olive orchard. The harvested olive's primary value was their oil. The oil was obtained by crushing the olives under the extreme weight of a heavy stone wheel. Do you know what *Gethsemane* means? It means "oil press" or "the place of the oil press." It was an appropriate place for him to have been in that moment. As its name suggests, Gethsemane was, for Jesus, a place of extreme pressure, he was being crushed by immense weight. He was sweating heavily, as if his blood were dripping off his face. Can you feel the strain? Can you imagine it?

Comparing the Two Gardens

By contrast, the Garden of Eden was beautiful and luxurious. But the garden of Gethsemane was stressful, troubled, and filled with pressure. While Adam lived in peace and divine harmony, Jesus prayed where he was forced to deal with his human emotions and personal struggles.

Adam's sin in the Garden of Eden separated him from God. Jesus's obedience in Gethsemane restored man to God, and brought us us back to that perfect fellowship. Jesus in Gethsemane became our solution for being separated from God. Consider these two men in symbolism:

	Adam Garden of Eden	Jesus Garden of Gethsemane
Symbolism of garden	Paradise	Pressure
Purpose	To care for the garden	To sacrifice himself for all mankind
Experience in the garden	Simple, peaceful, comfortable	Challenging, stressful, painful

Did Adam's life of luxury equip him for the challenges he faced? How did he do in his moment of trial? Consider these points:

1. He failed in temptation.
2. His garden of light was surrendered for a world of darkness.
3. His failure ushered sin and judgment into the world.

Was Jesus ready? How did his life prepare him for when he was tested? That moment in the garden wasn't his first time to be severely tested. While in the desert, he faced Satan's temptations. Satan tempted Jesus to satisfy his needs and tempted him to personal power, authority, and splendor. Was Jesus tempted to bypass his Father's will, to choose power and pleasure over the humble life that led to the cross? If Jesus had succumbed to those temptations, would there be a kingdom of light? Would the nations have found hope? Jesus was temped every day and in every way, not just once and not just by a piece of fruit. In those final hours of his life, how did Jesus handle his temptation to escape the cross?

1. He defeated Satan in the garden as he had in the desert.

2. His garden of extreme pressure would take him to the cross of great shame and suffering.

3. His victory over sin ushered mercy and grace into a broken and fallen world.

The Constant Struggle

My life often wavers between Adam's amazing garden and the Messiah's place of pressure. The first garden ends with sin and frustration. The second one ends in victory and peace. How ironic. Each day, I'm challenged to face the fact that I am Adam, a fallen and broken sinner. But then I'm lifted up, and elevated in praise to God for the sacrifice made by Jesus, my Messiah. In him, I am forgiven by grace, redeemed in mercy, and cleansed by the blood of the Lamb.

In the tale of two gardens, the first man's failure was redeemed by the second man's success. Jesus became our solution. He solved our problem with sin and separation. He succeeded where every man and every man's religion has failed.

> Again, the gift of God is not like the result of the one man's sin: The judgment followed one sin and brought condemnation, but the gift followed many trespasses and brought justification. For if, by the trespass of the one man, death reigned through that one man, how much more will those who receive God's abundant provision of grace and of the gift of righteousness reign in life through the one man, Jesus Christ. (Romans 5:16–17)

For Us Today

I love my country. The United States is my home and remains the only place I want to live. I've seen some of the world: My family spent four years in England when I was young. I've done mission work in some of Mexico's poorest areas. I've preached in China. I've enjoyed the incredible landscapes and mountain wonders of Canada. I've traveled over Israel and seen the disparity between the economic success of the Jews and the relative poverty of the Palestinians. I have worshiped in Jerusalem with Jews and Gentiles alike, praising Yeshua ben Joseph.

But the country that's had the greatest spiritual impact on my life is Haiti. For several years, I was joyously blessed to work for a ministry called Hope for Haiti's Children, or HFHC. HFHC is a nonprofit ministry providing Christian education, orphan care, medical support, crisis relief, and other related services to the Haitian people. Each and every mission trip was impactful, never failing to provide new experiences and lasting memories.

The mountains of central Haiti rise up in stark contrast to the crowded urban conditions below. Port-au-Prince is a bustling, dusty, smoky, and hugely overcrowded city. But there is a transformation once you get up into the mountains. The temperature starts to drop, there are far fewer people, and the landscape changes with flowers and trees. And it's calmer up there, more pastoral and serene.

On one such trip, seven of us were packed into a four-wheel drive vehicle and were slowly working our way up a treacherous narrow mountain path to visit some village schools. After our last visit of the day, the school's administrator, who was also the preacher for the little church which housed the school, invited us to his home for dinner.

His house was just down the dirt road; it was a small place of maybe 250 square feet. It was made of cinder block with a rusty, corrugated tin roof. It had two small rooms in the front and two in the back, all sparsely furnished. It did not have a bathroom or running water or electricity. Food was prepared outside. Obviously, there was no refrigerator, oven, microwave, or any appliances of any kind.

In addition to the seven of us, the preacher had invited some relatives to join them for dinner. There were maybe twenty-five or thirty Haitians. As we gathered around the little front porch, he welcomed us with gracious words and worded a sweet prayer, which was all interpreted for those of us not speaking Haitian Creole. We felt awkward that they had gone to great effort and expense. We knew the preacher couldn't afford to feed all of us.

His wife had cooked all day, preparing fried chicken legs, lettuce salad with tomato wedges, fried plantains, and white rice. We were invited to fill our plates. By Haitian standards, it was a feast fit for a king. But it was so humbling. We didn't put very much on our plates. We couldn't. It didn't feel right. We took small portions and risked offending the cook. She thought of us as rich Americans who were accustomed to eating large meals. They even insisted we go back to get more; but this time, she served us and piled our plates with her food. It broke our hearts. You see, they had to walk five miles each way to buy all the food. They knew we couldn't drink their water, so they bought bottles of Sprite to have with dinner. While we ate, not one of our hosts, not even a child, was allowed to get any food until the Americans had eaten all they wanted. We hid our embarrassment and our tears. They wouldn't have understood.

Never have I been served by such loving people with such generous hearts. They knew our financial resources made their school possible. They understood that our clinics with the doctors, dentists, optometrists, and nurses were their only medical support. They loved us for helping, and this dinner was their way of showing appreciation. The preacher thanked God in his prayer for the honor of having us in his home. He was very pleased to host such important Americans.

After a couple of hours, it was getting dark, and we needed to leave. We said our good-byes, never a quick thing with the Haitians. There were words of blessing, kisses on each cheek, and still a sense that we were somehow offending them by leaving so soon! As we drove off, the children ran behind our SUV, yelling and laughing and saying good-bye.

So here is a modern application of the tale of two gardens. The first garden is my home in Houston, and the second garden is the home up on the Haitian mountain. The first one is beautiful, and filled with wondrous things. The second one is dark, hot, and pitiful. My home is very comfortable and convenient. His home—well, it wasn't any of these things. The people living the poorest place, the place that provides them with so little, was the place of grace and overwhelming generosity. The people living in the riches of America often struggle to put God first and others second. There are the two gardens with their messages for us today.

Conclusion

Adam had it all—a beautiful home, a sweet abundance, a perfect wife, and a perfect life. But somehow it wasn't enough. He just needed that one piece of fruit for his life to be complete. Jesus prayed in Gethsemane, on his knees, perhaps with his face in the dirt, humble, struggling, reaching out for his Father's help. It seems like it's always the place of extreme pressure that gets us to do the Father's will.

Which garden are you living in? As appealing as life in Eden may seem, is it not true that the truly important things are most often realized in the garden of great pressure? That which is obtained too easily is often esteemed too lightly?

It's a tale of two gardens. The first one ended with us in desperate need of a Savior. The second one ended with our greatest need getting met. Jesus accepted his Father's will. He went with the soldiers. They beat him half to death. They nailed him to a cross. They despised and hated him. His garden of the oil press prepared him well for the hill of Calvary. Thank you, Jesus.

12

Seven Statements
That Changed the World

Introduction

My earliest memory of death came from a funeral my family attended when I was seven years old. One of Dad's relatives had passed away, so Mom packed us up, and off we went. We arrived a day early to support the family. The funeral would be the following day. When we got to their house, we went inside and joined the friends and family who were there to extend their sympathies. They led us into the living room, and there it was, the open casket. I had never seen a dead person before. People were chatting and eating food. *How can they stand there and eat with a dead person in the room?* I thought to myself.

My mother had prepared me for my manners of the day: "Ricky, mind your manners. Sit still and don't make any noise." So I sat on a chair in a corner, struggling with a plate of food on my knees. It was old people's food. Not hotdogs, mac and cheese, or PB&J. There was a long table with bowls of vegetables and casseroles and ham. I remember there being a lot of ham. I didn't like the food they gave me, and I didn't like the place I had to sit to eat it. I especially didn't like doing all of this with a dead person ten feet away. I wouldn't remember much about the funeral, but I would never forget the dead person in the living room.

At the tender age of seven, I had no way of knowing that God would call me to ministry, but He did. How ironic that the little boy so affected that day by death would end up sitting with grieving families—and doing so while struggling to balance a plate of food on his knees. There would still be a lot of ham.

Jesus and Death

Was Jesus called upon to provide this kind of comfort? Wasn't it after Lazarus was buried that Jesus finally went to Bethany? He went and wept with those who were weeping. He cried even though he knew he was about to call Lazarus from the tomb. He allowed his friend to die, doing nothing to intervene, knowing full well the kind of pain and confusion it would cause to the people he loved. They didn't understand why Jesus stayed away, choosing not to heal their brother. They were left hurting, confused, and grieving. And then soon, it would be his turn to die.

How was his death? Was it swift and painless? No, his death was slow and agonizingly painful. How did he manage his six hours on the cross? Did he suffer in silence? If you were dying and had only six hours to live, what would you want to say and to whom would you speak? The Bible records that Jesus spoke seven times while on the cross. What he chose to say in the final hours of his life was remarkably poignant.

In his last hours leading up to cross, Jesus experienced some serious setbacks. Judas approached him in the garden with a kiss of betrayal. The soldiers came with weapons to arrest him as if he and his disciples were a group of well-armed mercenaries. To fulfill scripture, Jesus made sure a few swords were present, but that was all. When Peter attacked, Jesus put an immediate end to the hostilities, even healing Malchus, restoring his ear that Peter had cut off. Jesus watched a majority of his disciples run away from him in fear.

Later, as the Jewish guards abused him, he knew Peter was outside, warming himself by the fire and denying even knowing him. The Roman soldiers would end up with Jesus, and he would endure the scourging, the beatings, the crown of thorns, and the cross. Jesus had every opportunity to express anger, bitterness, and deep disappointment to those who had abused, betrayed, and abandoned him. Did he?

Here are three examples of what Jesus could have expressed while on the cross, but didn't.

To the Roman Soldiers

Did he verbally attack his accusers out of anger? Would you blame him if he had? They beat him nearly to death, stripped him naked, stuck thorns on his head, and hammered spikes into his body. Then they lifted him up on a cross of shame and ridicule. Did he rage against them, seek revenge, or blame them for his unjust pain? The answer is no, he didn't. In fact, as Isaiah prophesied, he didn't open his mouth even once with words of hate or ugliness.

> He was oppressed and afflicted, yet he did not open his mouth; he was led like a lamb to the slaughter, and as a sheep before her shearers is silent, so he did not open his mouth. (Isaiah 53:7)

> But I am a worm and not a man, scorned by everyone, despised by the people. All who see me mock me; they hurl insults, shaking their heads. (Psalm 22:6–7)

To the Crowd Around Him

Maybe Jesus would use his time on the cross to speak words of resentment for having lived in poverty. Jesus didn't own lands, houses, or fields of grain. Jesus didn't possess orchards of olive trees, figs, dates, or vineyards of grapes. Did he have a large wardrobe of rich and beautiful clothes? No, at the moment of the cross, he owned nothing. He had never owned anything. He once said that the Son of man had no place to lay his head. The only possession Jesus had at the time of his death was the robe he was wearing. And they took that away from him. Did it bother him that those who drove the nails were gambling for the clothes off his back? But no, he expressed no animosity or resentment. His purpose wasn't to acquire goods and wealth. In fact, it was prophesied in Psalm 22 that the Messiah would die in poverty.

> When the soldiers crucified Jesus, they took his clothes, dividing them into four shares, one for each of them, with the undergarment remaining. This garment was seamless, woven in one piece from top to bottom. "Let's not tear it," they said to one another. "Let's decide by lot who will get it." This happened that the scripture might be fulfilled which said, "They divided my garments among them, and cast lots for my clothes." (John 19:22–24)

To His Loyal Disciples

Perhaps Jesus would express his disappointment in his disciples for denying, rejecting, and abandoning him. They weren't there to hear it, even if Jesus were to say such things. But if he wanted to, Jesus could have railed in anger, spewing venom at Peter and Judas and to the nine for running off. But no, Jesus didn't express any of these words. Psalm 22:11

well captures Jesus's attitude on the cross. "Do not be far from me, for trouble is near and there is no one to help" (Psalm 22:11).

Jesus's statements weren't about revenge, hatred or personal disappointment. Since his life was devoted to fulfilling the law, the psalms, and the prophets, does it make sense that his final words would reflect that devotion? Even on the cross, Jesus was fulfilling the scriptures and completing his mission.

For six hours, he hung on the cross; and while he did, he spoke seven times. Here are those statements, in the order in which he said them:

1. "Father, forgive them. They do not know what they are doing."
2. "Today you will be with me in paradise."
3. "Woman, behold your son. Son, behold your mother."
4. "My God, my God, why have you forsaken me?"
5. "I thirst."
6. "It is finished."
7. "Father, into your hands, I commit my spirit."

I believe that all seven of Jesus's final statements came from Psalm 22, the psalm that is known as the death psalm.[1] For example, Psalm 22:6–7 mentions his being scorned and despised by the people. They would hurl insults and mock him regarding his trusting the Lord for deliverance. See how these prophesies were fulfilled in Matthew 27:

> But I am a worm and not a man, scorned by men and despised by the people. All who see me hurl

insults, shaking their heads: He trusts in the Lord; let the Lord rescue him. Let him deliver him since he delights in him. (Psalm 22:6–7)

Those who passed by hurled insults at him, shaking their heads and saying, "You who are going to destroy the temple and build it in three days, save yourself! Come down from the cross, if you are the Son of God?"

In the same way the chief priests, the teachers of the law and elders mocked him. "He saved others," they said, "but he can't save himself! He is the King of Israel! Let him come down now from the cross, and we will believe in him. He trusts in God. Let God rescue him now if he wants him, for he said, 'I am the Son of God.'" (Matthew 27:39–43)

As we work through the seven statements, we will attempt to match them with specific verses from Psalm 22. For even on the cross—with the physical, emotional, and mental trauma—Jesus was still fulfilling scripture. He was still serving and caring for others.

13

The Seven Statements: Jesus and Others

In his first three statements, Jesus reached out to help and to serve those around him. He spoke words of forgiveness for some soldiers, words of salvation for a thief, and words of loving care for his mother.

His First Statement

> Father forgive them, for they do not know what they are doing. (Luke 23:34)

His first statement was spoken to the Father to seek forgiveness for "them." But who were they? In the context of Luke 23, the request is for those who hammered the nails and gambled for his clothes. He was asking the Father to forgive the Roman soldiers.

The Story

Jesus, the Lamb of God, would be sacrificed during the celebration of Passover. At the end of that week—after he had taught, healed, and done remarkable things—it was time to begin his passion. It was time for the garden of Gethsemane and his cross.

Jesus spent the night on trial. By morning, his accusers and judges had a verdict: Jesus was guilty. The chief priests and the elders of the people came to the decision to put Jesus to death. They bound him, led him away and handed him over to Pilate, the governor (Matthew 27:1–2). Through Pilate, they got what they wanted, a painful death for Jesus of Nazareth—a death that was public, shameful, and humiliating. Crucifixion wasn't Jewish; it was Roman. The Romans didn't invent the cross, but they perfected it.

The death of Jesus of Nazareth became a Roman matter. While in their custody, the soldiers did the following to Jesus, according to Matthew:

1. Flogged him with the scourge (ch. 27, v. 26)
2. Stripped off his clothes and put on the scarlet robe (ch. 26, v. 28)
3. Put the crown of thorns on his head and a staff in his right hand (ch. 27, v. 29)
4. Mocked him (ch. 27, v. 29)
5. Spit on him (ch. 27, v. 30)
6. Struck him on the head repeatedly with the staff (ch. 27, v. 30)
7. Took off the robe, put his clothes back on him, led him to the cross (ch. 27, v. 31)

All of this happened before the first spike was hammered. The scourging alone left his body a bloody mess. Then he was forced to carry a section of the cross. How do you ask forgiveness for those who have treated you with such prejudice, hatred, and violence?

Notice that Jesus asked his Father to forgive them. Jesus didn't say to the soldiers, "I forgive you." He asked his Father to forgive them. I can't imagine having to watch my son be humiliated, tortured, and executed. And then, at the very worst of it, he looks me in the eye and says, "Dad, forgive them, don't hold this against them. They don't know what they are doing. Can you imagine Jesus on the cross, seeking forgiveness for those violent, pagan men.

From the Hebrew Text

What did David and Isaiah say about the Messiah?

> Dogs surround me, a pack of villains encircles me; they pierce my hands and my feet. All my bones are on display; people stare and gloat over me. They divide my clothes among them and cast lots for my garment. (Psalm 22:16–18)

> For to us a child is born, to us a son is given, and the government will be on his shoulders. And he will be called Wonderful Counselor, Mighty God, Everlasting Father, Prince of Peace. (Isaiah 9:6)

> But he was pierced for our transgressions, he was crushed for our iniquities; the punishment that bought us peace was upon him, and by his wounds we are healed. (Isaiah 53:5)

Our Messiah was the Prince of Peace. Like an olive in the press, he was crushed for our iniquities. He was oppressed and afflicted, and his wounds healed us. His punishment resulted in our peace.

"Father, forgive them, for they do not know what they are doing."

From the Greek Text

Paul wrote to the Ephesian church to elevate the Prince of Peace. He wrote that Jesus destroyed the barrier, the dividing wall of hostility, and made the two into one—that Jesus himself is our peace (Ephesians 2:13–14). Jesus understood the death he came to give. He knew his kingdom was not of this world; it wasn't going to be about anger, revenge, and violence. In John 18:36, Jesus said, "My kingdom is not of this world. If it were, my servants would fight to prevent my arrest by the Jews. But now my kingdom is of a different place." Let's not forget what he said in Gethsemane when Peter pulled out his sword and attacked Malchus.

> "Put your sword back in its place," Jesus said to him, "for all who draw the sword will die by the sword. Do you think I cannot call on my Father, and he will at once put at my disposal more than twelve legions of angels?" (Matthew 26:52–53)

Jesus had every reason to be anything but forgiving. He could have instigated a rebellion, even a war. He could have called upon an angelic army of soldiers. But instead, with only hours to live, he found the compassion to seek forgiveness for the Roman soldiers who defiled and debased him.

There he was on the cross, naked and bleeding, the perfect Son of God. He was still teaching, still serving, and showing the way to heal a broken world.

The Second Statement

> I tell you the truth, today you will be with me in paradise. (Luke 23:43)

Conservative believers sometimes struggle with this statement. Does it seem that Jesus was offering "cheap grace" to this thief on the cross? Who was this man? What do we know about him? Matthew said of him in chapter

27, verse 38: "Two robbers were crucified with him, one on his right and one on his left."

Robber is the word that Matthew used for these men. The Hebrew word meant "a robber or thief." It's from a root word meaning "to plunder." Luke used the word *criminal*. In Hebrew, it's defined as "a wrongdoer, an evildoer, a malefactor." A malefactor is a person who "violates the law, a person who does evil, especially towards another." Since they were being crucified, it's likely that these men were Jewish. Rome didn't sentence their own citizens to crucifixion; it was against their law.

Jesus had already asked the Father to forgive the soldiers, and they were pagans. Now he offered paradise to a criminal, a Jewish thief. Really? Some part of me wants to side with the conservatives on this one. Why should this criminal receive such grace? It was prophesied that he would be counted with the criminals, so there he was, hanging on a cross between two thieves.

From the Hebrew Text

Dogs have surrounded me; a band of evil men has encircled me. (Psalm 22:16)

Therefore I will give him a portion among the great, and he will divide the spoils with the strong, because he poured out his life unto death, and was numbered with the transgressors. For he bore the sin of many, and made intercession for the transgressors. (Isaiah 53:12)

From the Greek Text

Jesus was numbered with the transgressors. He was crucified as a common criminal. But he wasn't a criminal. Nor did he treat the others like criminals.

> One of the criminals who hung there hurled insults at him: "Aren't you the Christ? Save yourself and us!" But the other criminal rebuked him. "Don't you fear God," he said, "since you are under the same sentence? We are punished justly, for we are getting what our deeds deserve. But this man has done nothing wrong." Then he said, "Jesus, remember me when you come into your kingdom." Jesus answered him, "I tell you the truth, today you will be with me in paradise." (Luke 23:39–43)

The Gospels record many examples of Jesus forgiving sins. Remember the woman caught in adultery? "Neither do I condemn you, go your way and leave your life of sin" (John 8:1–11). He offered Living Water to a Samaritan woman who had five previous husbands and apparently was with a man not her husband. He offered Living Water to her entire Samaritan village (John 4:1–15). He forgave the sins of the paralytic who was lowered through the roof (Luke 5:17–20). He called Levi to repentance and discipleship (Luke 5:27–31). Jesus forgave the sins of the sinful woman who anointed his feet (Luke 7:36–48).

That he would offer salvation to this thief isn't unusual at all. He had been offering forgiveness throughout his ministry. Whenever he recognized faith, a broken and contrite heart, he responded with heaven's gifts. Clearly, the thief believed in Jesus, the Messiah.

This is our Lord and Savior who came not to be served but to serve and to give his life a ransom for many (Mark 10:45). Even on the cross, he was looking for lost sheep.

"Today you will be with me in paradise."

Thank you, Jesus.

The Third Statement

His third statement was laced with loving concern for his mother. Jesus revealed his great humanity, offering to her and to John his heartfelt words of devotion to family.

> When Jesus saw his mother there, and the disciple whom he loved standing nearby, he said to his mother, "Dear woman, here is your son," and to the disciple, "Here is your mother." (John 19:26–27)

How amazing that Jesus did that while hanging on the cross! It amazes me that while he was suffering, he was still thinking of others: the soldiers, the thief, and his mother. God was his Heavenly Father. He was conceived through the Holy Spirit, but Jesus came into this world through a human mother. It's very sweet and touching that he made sure she was taken care of, not just fed and given a place to live, but given a new son to love her. It was even prophesied from the Psalms and Isaiah that our Messiah, would have a mother.

From the Hebrew Text

> Yet you brought me out of the womb; you made me trust in you even at my mother's breast. From birth I was cast upon you; from my mother's womb you have been my God. (Psalm 22:9)

> Therefore the Lord himself will give you a sign: The
> virgin will be with child and will give birth to a son,
> and will call him Immanuel. (Isaiah 7:14)

Let's take a brief look at Jesus and Mary. What kind of relationship did they have? Were they close? Was this, in any way, a normal mother-and-son relationship?

From the Greek Text

> This is how the birth of Jesus Christ came about: His
> mother Mary was pledged to be married to Joseph, but
> before they came together, she was found to be with
> child through the power of the Holy Spirit. Because
> Joseph her husband was a righteous man and did not
> want to expose her to public disgrace, he had in mind
> to divorce her quietly. (Matthew 1:18–19)

Here is what happened with Mary. She nearly lost her betrothed over this pregnancy. Joseph thought she had done the unthinkable, the unforgivable. The Messiah hadn't even been born, yet he was causing her heartache.

When the time came, Mary and Joseph traveled to Bethlehem, and she delivered the deliverer. Not in a private, comfortable room but in a cold cave serving as a barn for draft animals. Jesus, the Bread of Life, was to be born in the place of bread, for *Bethlehem* means "house or place of bread." He was placed in a manger, not a wooden feeding trough, but a place that had been hewn out of the stone floor for feeding animals. Jesus's first bed was where the animals were fed.

"But Mary treasured up all these things and pondered them in her heart."

The sweet moments wouldn't last. Herod wanted to kill the newborn King, for he would have no rivals. Having been warned, Mary and Joseph fled to Egypt and remained there until it was safe to return. It was prophesied that God would call his son from Egypt (Hosea 11:1).

The family returned to their hometown of Nazareth, and there Jesus was raised until he turned thirty.

Luke 2 records that when Jesus was twelve, the family went to Jerusalem for Passover. After the celebrations, the caravan headed back to Galilee. It was a full day's travel before Mary realized Jesus wasn't with the group. Is there any greater panic than the moment a parent realizes their child is missing? So they hurried back to Jerusalem. They searched for three days but couldn't find him. Finally they looked in the temple, and there he was, in a Bible study with the rabbis. He was twelve. Imagine Mary's angst. She said, "Son, why have you treated us like this? Your father and I have been anxiously searching for you."

They went back to Nazareth and Jesus was obedient to them. When he reached the age of thirty, he launched his ministry.

> But his mother treasured all these things in her heart.
> (Luke 2:51)

Was she there to hear him teach the Sermon on the Mount? Did she see him calm the storms on the Sea of Galilee? Was she overflowing with parental pride when her son cleansed the lepers, restored the blind, and healed the sick? Did she rejoice with those delivered from demons? Imagine how she must have felt when she heard about him walking on the water, or when he fed the five thousand. Was she wistful seeing him with the little children, knowing he would never present her with grandchildren?

Did she know that when he launched his ministry, he only had a few years to live? How close was she when they mocked him, stripped him naked, and beat him? Was she able to watch the scourging? How awful it must have been to hear her fellow countrymen scream for her son's death. A song asks the question, "Were you there when they crucified my Lord?" Well, his mother was.

Do you have a sense of what it cost Mary to be the Messiah's mother? There she was at the cross, looking at her son, trying to be strong while watching him die. It's been said that no parent should outlive their child. She did.

Jesus made sure she knew how much he loved her. He entrusted his mom to his closest disciple, to care for her when he no longer could. Can you see her? She's the woman struggling with a broken heart.

"Dear woman, behold your son."

14

The Seven Statements: Jesus and God

The Fourth Statement

The first three statements were spoken to, or on behalf of the soldiers, the thief, and his mother. His fourth statement was spoken to his Father: "My God, my God, why have you forsaken me?" The entire Psalm 22:1 verse reads:

> My God, my God, why have you forsaken me? Why are you so far from saving me, so far from the words of my groaning?

Jesus asked these sad and painful questions to His Father.

From the Hebrew Text

Did these words express Jesus's deepest sadness? "Why have you forsaken me?" Wouldn't we think that Jesus knew the answer to this question? Did the question come from a deeper place, a place of deep desperation? To be forsaken is to be abandoned, resulting in a deep sadness. Jesus was calling to his Father in a moment of great pain, but his Father wasn't listening, or wasn't responding. In that moment on the cross, was it like his Father had turned his back on him, refusing to help?

Remember, it was just the night before, in Gethsemane, that Jesus prayed for the cup to be taken from him. In the scriptures, cups can be containers of blessings or curses. For Jesus, his was not a cup from which he wanted to drink.[1] As Thomas W. Davis wrote, "Throughout scripture, as in the ancient Near East, the cup functions as a metaphor for an individual's fate."[2]

God was willing for him to drink the bitter cup of pain and sorrow. Jesus asked, God said no, and Jesus submitted to His Father. In that moment of his fourth statement, was Jesus struggling with the full implication of being forsaken, his total separation from his Father?

The word *forsaken* appears somewhat frequently in scripture. But it's usually in the context of man forsaking God. Scripture declares that God does not, has not, forsaken His people. He keeps His covenants. He blesses and rewards faith and obedience. He honors devotion to his Word. He lifts up those who seek Him.

> Though we are slaves, our God has not deserted [forsaken] us. (Ezra 9:9)

> Those who know your name will trust in you, for you, Lord, have never forsaken those who seek you. (Psalm 9:10)

This, of course, begs the question, If God is faithful—if He does not abandon, forget, or forsake us—then why did Jesus ask the question?

"My God, my God, why have you forsaken me?"

From the Greek Text

Theologically, I place this fourth statement in the context of Jesus becoming sin, of his taking on the sins of the world. The consequences of sin are well documented in scripture:

1. Adam sinned, and he was banished from Eden (Genesis 3:23).

2. Man desired evil, and a flood destroyed all but Noah and his family (Genesis 6–8).

3. Paul said, "For the wages of sin is death" (Romans 6:23).

Jesus became the scapegoat for all mankind. And like the scapegoats of old, Jesus also was led outside the city to die. Sin separates us from God. Sin is the opposite of holiness.

Jesus committed no sin, had no moral indiscretions. He was a lamb led to the slaughter, the perfect symbol of innocence and purity.

> We all, like sheep, have gone astray, each of us has turned to his own way; and the Lord has laid on him the iniquity of us all. He was oppressed and afflicted, yet he did not open his mouth; he was led like a lamb led to the slaughter. (Isaiah 53:6–7)

God knew we would need a perfect and holy sacrifice. He has always known. When God instigated the blood covenant nearly four thousand years ago, He knew the day would come when Jesus would have to stand for Abraham, for the lost sheep of Israel, and for the Gentiles. God's Son would have his blood poured out so none of us would have to. He didn't deserve it, but he submitted to it.

> Behold the Lamb of God who takes away the sin of the world. (John 1:29)

> God made him who had no sin to be sin for us, so that in him we might become the righteousness of God. (2 Corinthians 5:21)

Did Jesus feel the piercing sting of sin, the crushing weight of fallen man? While on the cross, did he fully know the consequences of man's failure? We know that Jesus was without sin; but on the cross, he knew the wages of all our indiscretions, moral weakness, and sinful disobedience. He suffered the consequences of sin from Adam to every one of us.

Perhaps Jesus worded his fourth statement to fulfill Psalm 22:1. But I believe he also said it to reveal to the Father how he felt and what he was thinking. In that moment, what else could he say?

"My God, my God, why have you forsaken me?"

15

The Seven Statements:
Jesus Finishes His Work

In his previous statements, Jesus spoke to others and then to his Father. His final statements were about completing things—fulfilling scripture, proclaiming his life and work to be finished, and committing his spirit to the Father.

The Fifth Statement

"I thirst."

From the moment he made his fifth statement, in John 19:38, how long had it been since he had something to drink? We don't really know; the text doesn't say. But it may have been the previous evening when he and his disciples shared their final meal. Jesus was arrested and then began the long night of his trial. Was he given anything to drink? Would the Jewish or Roman soldiers have cared?

It had been perhaps twelve to fifteen hours since Jesus shared the meal with the disciples. He had been beaten, scourged, and had already lost a lot of blood. So how thirsty was he? Was Jesus already suffering from dehydration before the first nail was hammered?

"I thirst."

Imagine that the source of Living Water had nothing to drink. Jesus offered Living Water to the Samaritan woman and offered it to anyone who would come to him and drink. Ezekiel envisioned the Holy Spirit as a river of life, transforming everything it touched. Even Moses was able to get the water and quench the thirst of those he led in the desert.

But the imagery is gut-wrenching. Jesus walked on water and turned water into wine. He had the blind man wash in the Pool of Siloam. But there was no water for the giver of life.

From the Hebrew Text

Jesus was close to death. But he still had work to do.

> My strength is dried up like a potsherd, and my tongue sticks to the roof of my mouth; you lay me in the dust of death. (Psalm 22:15)

> They put gall in my food and gave me vinegar for my thirst. (Psalm 69:21)

Jesus needed to fulfill the statements from Psalms 22 and 69, and he did.

> Later, knowing that all was now completed, and so that the Scripture would be fulfilled, Jesus said, "I am thirsty." A jar of wine vinegar was there, so they soaked a sponge in it, put the sponge on a stalk of the hyssop plant, and lifted it to Jesus' lips. (John 19:28–29)

Here are some insights about the wine vinegar and hyssop:

Hyssop

The hyssop plant is an herb, and it is found in a number of biblical texts, especially in the Old Testament. Hyssop was used by the priests to ceremonially clean someone with skin disease (Leviticus 14:1–7). It was also used in the cleansing of people, of houses, and had medicinal applications.[1]

The plant had a long stalk, and it may have been for that reason only that it was used with the sponge. But certainly there is consideration for both its medicinal value and spiritual symbolism that the hyssop stalk was used.[2]

Also, remember the original Passover night? The Jews were to sacrifice a lamb, take some of its blood, and apply it to their doorposts using hyssop stalks to apply the blood. In Psalm 51:7, David asked God to cleanse him with hyssop so he would be clean.[3]

Wine Vinegar and Gall

The value of the wine vinegar and gall was that it served as a mild painkiller, to dull the senses.

From the Greek Text

Notice that Jesus didn't ask for a drink, only that he was thirsty. In Matthew 27:34, Jesus was offered wine mixed with gall, which after tasting it, declined to have any more. He still had to be incredibly parched. Did he decline the drink because he wanted to feel the full effects of our sin? Jesus could have accepted the pain reliever, even just a little. But he didn't; he carried the pain, physically and spiritually, all the way. Clearly, his greater need was to fulfill everything written about him in the law, the psalms, and the prophets. His fifth statement of "I thirst" was more about Jesus completing his mission than getting something to drink.

In that moment, there couldn't have been much left of him. The scourging and spikes would have caused massive tissue damage. He would have been exhausted, bleeding out, and severely dehydrated. With nothing left to fulfill, it was time to finish what his Father had sent him to do—it was time for Jesus to die.

"I thirst."

The Sixth Statement

It is finished. (John 19:30)

From the Hebrew Text

They will proclaim his righteousness to a people yet unborn, for he has done it. (Psalm 22:31)

From the Greek Text

Jesus was ready to die. He had finished his mission.

When he had received the drink, Jesus said, "It is finished." With that he bowed his head and gave up his spirit. (John 19:30)

What did he mean when he said, "It is finished"? What does "it" refer to? Did he mean his life was finished or that the process of the cross was competed? Or was he referring to his ministry?

The word Jesus used for *finished* means "to end, complete, conclude, or accomplish." John recorded that Jesus knew that everything was completed (John 19:28).

The word *completed* is the same Greek word for *finished*. What did he finish? What was completed? He was born of woman, but he was born to die. He came to exchange his life for ours.

> For even the Son of Man did not come to be served,
> but to serve, and to give his life as a ransom for many.
> (Mark 10:45)

It's different for us. We don't live as if our greatest goal in life is to die. Our goals are realized in our living. Mostly we go out kicking, clawing, and screaming to stay in, to stay alive. But it wasn't like that for Jesus. His whole life was about dying to wash away the sins of the world. Remember what the angel said to Joseph?

> She will give birth to a son and you are to give him the
> name Jesus, because he will save his people from their
> sins. (Matthew 1:21)

Jesus, or *Yeshua*, means "save" or "the Lord is our salvation." I believe that when Yeshua, declared, "It is finished," he was referring to the plan of God for the salvation of the world. The plan created before time began. At the cross, God, through His Son, fulfilled the blood path, the blood covenant made with Abraham some 1800 years earlier (see chapter 1).

The cross was about the Anointed of God taking on the sins of mankind. He took your sins and mine and those of Zacchaeus and the Pan worshipers and the Ninevites and Jonah and those of the lost sheep of Israel. He even took the sins of those who screamed for His crucifixion. Jesus completed the blood covenant at the cross, and in that final moment, he finished the purpose of God.

> For God so loved the world, that He gave his one and
> only son, that whoever believes in him shall not perish
> but have eternal life. (John 3:16)

"It is finished."

The Seventh Statement

Father, into your hands I commit my spirit. (Luke 23:46)
  The full verse reads,

> Jesus called out in a loud voice, "Father, into your hands I commit my spirit." When he had said this, be breathed his last.

It seems likely that the final two statements overlap each other. In the sixth statement, after pronouncing, "It is finished," Jesus breathed his last. In his seventh statement, Jesus simply bowed his head and gave up his spirit. Perhaps the final words of Christ were, "It is finished. Father, into your hands, I commit my spirit." Then he bowed his head and breathed his last. To his very last moment, Jesus was completing and fulfilling the prophecies made about the Messiah.

From the Hebrew Text

> From you comes the theme of my praise in the great assembly; before those who fear you will I fulfill my vows. (Psalm 22:25)

This final verse of Psalm 22 may not be a direct prophecy, but I believe it applies to what Jesus was saying and achieving in his final moments. What was the theme of his praise in the great assembly? Was it that he had completed all that the Father had sent him to do? That he had fulfilled his vows? Does this refer to what Jesus said in John 17:4, "I have brought you glory on earth by finishing the work you gave me to do"?

From the Greek Text

When Jesus died, did heaven's angels weep? Matthew 27:45 recorded that darkness came over the land for three hours; of course darkness came over the land—it was a dark moment. A terrible battle was waged between the forces of light and the forces of darkness. The souls of all mankind were in the balance.

In the moment of his death, the curtain in the temple was torn in half from top to bottom (Matthew 27:51). Behind that curtain was where the Lord hovered over the Ark of the Covenant. The curtain served to separate the holy place from the most holy place. It also separated the holy God from the unholy people. No one was permitted to go behind the curtain save the high priest, and then only once a year. When Jesus died, the curtain was torn in half; not so that God could come out but to give all mankind a way in. As the author of Hebrews wrote: "Let us then approach the throne of grace with confidence; so that we may receive mercy and find grace to help us in our time of need" (Hebrews 4:16).

The Father, through his magnificent mercy welcomed each of us into His life. He set before us the goodness of His Grace, inviting us to join him in the splendor of His glory. The tearing of the temple's curtain was God calling us home. Our Father has been watching and waiting for our return.

> Joseph and Nicodemus, two of his disciples with apparent wealth and influence, obtained Pilate's permission to take charge of Jesus's body. They gently lowered him to the ground, removing the spikes and lifting the crown of thorns. They gently washed his pierced and bloody body and prepared him for burial.

Joseph of Arimathea volunteered his new, unused tomb. And so even in death, Jesus was still completing scripture.

"He was assigned a grave with the wicked, and with the rich in his death, though he had done no violence, nor was any deceit found in his mouth" (Isaiah 53:9).

"Into your hands, I commit my spirit."

16

It's Saturday Night in the Upper Room

The People at the Cross

What happened to all the people after Jesus died? Scripture doesn't mention how big the crowd was. But it does mention that his mother, Mary, was there, as were some other women who were disciples. John, the disciple whom Jesus loved, was there. A Roman centurion was there with his guards. The chief priests and rabbis were out at Golgotha. But what happened once it was all over; where did the people go?

Was there someone in charge saying something like, "Okay, folks, show's over. Nothing more to see here. Move it along." Luke recorded in 23:48 that once Jesus was dead, the crowds all went away. But some remained who would take charge of Jesus's body and arrange for his burial. Those were Joseph, a member of the council; Nicodemus, who came to him at night and was also from Galilee;[1] and the women from Galilee who were there at the crucifixion (Luke 23:50–56; John 3:1, 19:39).

Where Did They Go?

Did Jesus's enemies walk away, feeling smug for successfully orchestrating the death of their rival? Were they feeling clever for having kept themselves undefiled, getting the

Romans to execute Jesus? Did the soldiers go back to their barracks, the chief priests to the temple, and the rabbis to the synagogues? Were the people highly engaged in conversation about the earthquake, the split rocks, and the open tombs? Or did everyone just go home? Certainly they would be conscious of the time, for it was getting late in the day, and the Jews would want to get home for Passover.

What do we know of the apostles' whereabouts?

- At his arrest, nine deserted him and fled (Matthew 26:56).
- Peter denied Jesus, went out and wept, his presence unknown (Matthew 26:75).
- Judas ended his life (Matthew 27:1–5).
- John is with Mary and remains close to her (John 19:25–27).

After leaving the tomb, where did Mary go? Was she with the women of Galilee, staying in whatever home they returned to? Did John go with her? Where were Simon Peter and the nine?

It's Resurrection Eve

Imagine now that it's about 24 hours later; it's the evening after the weekly Sabbath. One by one, the disciples are slowly returning to Jerusalem and are looking for one another. John has remained faithfully at Mary's side. By our calendars, it was Saturday night. Were they gathering together in the upper room?

If they were all together in the upper room, what were they doing? Did Peter remember the words of Jesus that after he returned from his denials that he should strengthen his brothers (Luke 22:31)? Did they discuss what happened at Gethsemane? Were the apostles second-guessing themselves, thinking they should have fought harder to prevent his arrest? Surely they were confused about Jesus telling them to put their swords away. Why would Jesus say to take swords if he wasn't going to fight? Did they recall the text that prophesied how the Messiah would be numbered with the transgressors? Did any of this make sense? Were they flabbergasted when Jesus surrendered to the soldiers? It must have been very confusing for the disciples. Did it seem to them that Jesus gave up, threw in the towel?

Or were they recalling his words about rising on the third day? Were they deep in prayer about his resurrection? He told them over and over that he would rise from the dead. Did they believe? Did they dare to hope? Were they counting down the hours until the end of the three days? Or were they just discouraged and defeated? Was there a round of finger-pointing, playing the blame game? Was there debate about who abandoned Jesus first?

Imagine Mary walking in to the upper room, with all of them engaged with all that was on their hearts and minds. Was she angry with the nine for running off? Did she avoid making eye contact with Peter for denying her son? Did she resent him for having pledged his life to Jesus, even to death? Did they weep together, unburdening the guilt and shame of their crushing failure?

I can imagine Peter walking over to Mary with a broken heart and humbly begging her forgiveness. Did he also apologize to John for leaving him? Would the other disciples, having watched Peter and Mary, follow his example and seek her forgiveness? In that moment could they have any idea, any way to imagine how their lives were just hours away from being changed forever? Any way of knowing what was about to happen?

Early the next morning some women went to the tomb with the spices they had prepared. But they rushed back, out of breath, to tell the others that the stone was rolled back, the soldiers were as dead men, and a messenger in radiant splendor had pronounced, "He is not here. He is risen." The eternal plan of God was finally, and gloriously, about to be unfolded to the entire world.

The Fulfillment of God's Plan

The resurrection of the the Anointed One has lit up the world for two thousand years. But the message of the empty tomb wasn't something that started at Joseph's tomb. No, the plan began before the creation of the world. The plan went active the moment Adam and Eve took the bite. The plan launched forward when God engaged with Abram in the blood path. Then God came near when a teenage girl gave birth on a cold and starry night.

In going back to the beginning, we are led to the plan of salvation in Jesus of Nazareth, the Son of David, the Son of God. We need to honor who he is and all he has done. Be encouraged to love him more, to get better connected, and to serve him better. Decide to be a disciple who digs deeper into the text. The Word of God is amazing, beautiful, and rich beyond treasure.[2]

Conclusion

The journey that led me to write this book continues to lead me. There is a rekindling of passion for the Word and a closer relationship with Jesus. His divine purpose—so beautifully painted by those who lived so long ago—comes alive when the law, the prophets, and the psalms are seen alongside the teachings of Christ. We must keep the flames burning bright both in our hearts and our minds. Don't let it become something less. Please consider these well-worded thoughts of Joshua Heschel:

> It is customary to blame secular science and anti-religious philosophy for the eclipse of religion in modern society. It would be more honest to blame religion for its own defeats. Religion declined not because it was refuted but because it became irrelevant, dull, oppressive, and insipid. When faith is completely replaced by creed, worship by discipline, love by habit; when the crisis of today is ignored because of the splendor of the past; when faith becomes an heirloom rather that a living fountain; when religion speaks only in the name of authority rather than with the voice of compassion, its message becomes meaningless.[3]

There is more to following Jesus than just practicing religion. There is more to the Living Water of the Spirit than the rules and traditions of men. There is the magnificent Messiah, full of grace and mercy, who is the way, the truth, and the life.

He fulfilled it all, accomplished everything, and he finished for us.

> And we, who with unveiled faces all reflect the Lord's glory, are being transformed into his likeness with ever-increasing glory, which comes from the Lord, who is the Spirit. (2 Corinthians 3:18)

Jesus, our Messiah.

Bibliography

Anderson, Lynn. *They Smell Like Sheep: Spiritual Leadership for the 21st Century*. West Monroe, LA: Howard Publishing Company, 1997.

Bacchiocchi, Samuele. *God's Festivals in Scripture and History: Part 2 The Fall Festivals*. Berrien Springs, MI: Biblical Perspectives, 2001.

Barnes, Ian. *The Historical Atlas of Judaism*. New York, NY: Chartwell Books Inc., 2009.

Belibtreu, Erika. "Grisly Assyrian Record of Torture and Death." *Biblical Archaeology Society* (Jan/Feb 1991). http://www.cojs.org/pdf/grisly_assyrian.pdf

Berkowitz, Miriam, C. *Taking the Plunge: A Practical and Spiritual Guide to the Mikveh*. Jerusalem, Israel: The Schechter Institute of Jewish Studies, 2009.

Bible History Online. "Ancient Tax Collector" (weblog post). http://www.bible-history.com/sketches/ancient/tax-collector.html

Brickner, David. "Finding Jesus in the Feast of Tabernacles." http://www.cbn.com/spirituallife/biblestudyand theology/jewishroots/feast_of_tabernacles_jews_for_jesus_david_brickner.aspx

Brown, Michael, L. *The Real Kosher Jesus: Revealing the Mysteries of the Hidden Messiah*. Lake Mary, FL: Front Line Charisma Media/Charisma House Book Group, 2012.

Boyarin, Daniel. *The Jewish Gospels: The Story of the Jewish Christ*. New York, NY: The New Press, 2012.

The Holy Bible, New International Version. Nashville, TN: Broadman & Holman Publishers, 1996.

Bivin, David. *New Light on the Difficult Words of Jesus: Insights from His Jewish Context*. Holland, MI: En-Gedi Resource Center Inc., 2007.

Brooks, Carol. "The Feasts of Israel." http://www.inplainsite. org/html/seven_feasts_of_israel.html

Buxbaum, Yitzhak. "Torah Teachings: Needed: Women with the Holy Spirit." *The Jewish Spiritual Journal* 1 (December 4, 1999).

Cartan, William. *The Christian's Manual*. London, England: Williams and Norgate, (1876).

Collins, Steven M. "Jonah—The Misunderstood Prophet" (weblog post). http://www.stevenmcollins.com/articles/ jonah-the-misunderstood-prophet/.

Davis, Edward B. "A Modern Jonah" (weblog post). December 1, 1990. http://www.reasons.org/ articles/a-modern-jonah

Davis, W. Thomas. "Cup." *Baker's Evangelical Dictionary of Biblical Theology*. http://www.biblestudytools.com/ dictionaries/bakers-evangelical-dictionary/cup.html

Diehl, T.H. *Biblical History: Old Testament*. Philadelphia, PA: James B. Rodgers Printing Co., 1884.

Duffield, Guy, P. *Hand-Book of Bible Lands*. Grand Rapids, MI: Baker Book House, 1960.

Edersheim, Alfred. *The Temple: Its Ministry and Services.* Grand Rapids, MI: William Eerdmans Publishing Company, 1958.

Eerdmans Publishing Company. *International Standard Bible Encyclopedia.* Grand Rapids, MI: William B. Eerdmans Publishing Company, 1939.

Flusser, David. *Judaism and the Origins of Christianity.* Jerusalem, Israel: The Hebrew University Magnes Press, 1988.

Flusser, David and Steven R. Notley. *The Sage from Galilee: Rediscovering Jesus' Genius.* Jerusalem, Israel: The Hebrew University Magnes Press, 1997.

"Follow the Rabbi." The Lord Is My Shepherd (weblog post). http://v2.followtherabbi.com/journey/faith-lesson/the-lord-is-my-shepherd

Gallups, Carl. *The Rabbi Who Found Messiah: The Story of Yitzhak Kaduri and His Prophesies of the End Time.* Washington, D.C.: WND Books Inc., 2013.

Garlow, James & Price, Robin M. (2013). *The Blood Covenant: The Story of God's Extraordinary Love for You.* (3rd ed.). Kansas City, KS: Beacon Hill Press.

Goodman, Philip. "On This Day of Judgment." In *The Rosh Hashanah Anthology.* Philadelphia, PA: The Jewish Publication Society of America, 1970.

Gordon, Nehemia. *The Hebrew Yeshua vs. the Greek Jesus: New Light on the Seat of Moses from Shem-Tov's Hebrew Matthew.* Chicago: Hilkiah Press, 2005.

Greenberg, Irving. *The Jewish Way: Living the Holidays.* New York, NY: Summit Books, 1988.

Henry, Matthew. *Matthew Henry's Commentary on the Whole Bible*. Iowa Falls, IA: World Bible Publishers, 1986.

Heschel, Abraham. *Joshua, God in Search of Man: A Philosophy of Judaism*. New York, NY: Farrar, Straus, and Giroux, 1955.

"Passover." Jewish Encyclopedia. http://www.jewish encyclopedia.com/articles/11933-passover

Kaiser, Walter, C. Jr. *The Messiah in the Old Testament: Studies in Old Testament Biblical Theology*. Grand Rapids, MI: Zondervan Publishing House, 1995.

Kent, Charles F. *Biblical Geography and History*. New York, NY: Charles Scribner's Sons, 1911.

Klein, Isaac. *A Guide to Jewish Religious Practice*. New York and Jerusalem: The Jewish Theological Seminary of America, 1979.

Lehrman, Rabbi S.M. *The Jewish Festivals*. London: Shapiro, Valentine & Co., 1956.

Masterman, E.W.G. "Olive Tree in the International Standard Bible Encyclopedia" International Standard Bible Encyclopedia Online. http://www.international-standardbible.com/O/olive-tree.html

McDougall, Heather. "The Pagan Roots of Easter | Heather McDougall." The Guardian. 2010. http://www.theguardian.com/commentisfree/belief/2010/apr/03/easter-pagan-symbolism

Moseley, PhD. Ron. *Yeshua: A Guide to the Real Jesus and the Original Church*. Clarksville, MD: Lederer Books, Messianic Jewish Publishers, 1996.

Natan, Yoel. *The Jewish Trinity: When Rabbis Believed in the Father, Son, and Holy Spirit.* Colorado Springs, CO: CreateSpace Independent Publishing Platform, 2003.

Palaia, Ariela. "What Is Mdirash?" About.com Religion & Spirituality. (weblog post). http://judaism.about.com/od/glossary/g/midrash.htm

Parsons, John J. "The Jewish Holidays: Understanding the Appointed Times." (weblog post). 2015. http://www.hebrew4christians.com/Holidays/holidays.html

Roberts, Mark D. "The Seven Last Words of Christ; Reflections for Holy Week." (weblog post). 2015. http://www.patheos.com/blogs/markdroberts/series/the-seven-last-words-of-christ-reflections-for-holy-week/

Roth, Andrew Gabriel. *Aramaic English New Testament.* Sedro-Woolley, WA: Netzari Press LLC, 2008.

Rydelnik, Michael. *The Messianic Hope: Is the Hebrew Bible Really Messianic?* Nashville, TN: B&H Publishing Group, 2010.

Schneider, Luziuss. "The Messiah in the 7 Biblical Feasts." (weblog post). February 1, 2000. http://luziusschneider.com/Papers/JewishFeasts.htm

Schurer, Emil. *A History of the Jewish People: In the Time of Jesus Christ.* Peabody, MA: Hendrickson Publishers, 2010.

"Gethsemane." (weblog post). See The Holy Land. 2009. http://www.seetheholyland.net/gethsemane/

Smith, James E. *Old Testament Survey Series.* Joplin, MO: College Press Publishing Company, 1995.

Smith, Malcolm. *The Power of the Blood Covenant: Uncover the Secret Strength in God's Eternal Oath.* Tulsa, OK: Harrison House, Inc., 2002.

Stedman, Ray C. "Jonah: The Reluctant Ambassador." (weblog post). May 22, 1966. http://www.pbc.org/system/message_files/3128/0232.html

Stern, David H. *Jewish New Testament Commentary.* Clarksville, MD: Jewish New Testament Publications, Inc., 1992.

"Fertility Cults of Canaan." (weblog post). That the World May Know Ministries. https://www.thattheworldmayknow.com/fertility-cults-of-canaan

"Biblical Covenants." (weblog post). That the World May Know Ministries. https://www.thattheworldmayknow.com/biblical-covenants

Trumbull, Clay H. *The Blood Covenant.* Philadelphia, PA: John D. Wattles & Co., 1885.

Trumbull, H. Clay. "Jonah in Nineveh." *Journal of Biblical Literature.* 11, no. 1 (1892): 53 DOI: 10.2307/3259078.

Tverberg, Lois. *Walking In The Dust of Rabbi Jesus: How The Jewish Words of Jesus Can Change Your Life.* Grand Rapids, MI: Zondervan Publishing, 2012.

Vanderkam, James & Flint, Peter. *The Meaning of the Dead Sea Scrolls: The Significance for Understanding the Bible, Judaism, Jesus, and Christianity.* T&T New York, NY: Clark International, 2002.

"What Does Leaven Represent in the Scriptures?" (weblog post). http://www.letusreason.org/Biblexp184.htm

Winter, Naphtali. *The High Holy Days.* New York, NY: Leon Amiel Publishing, 1973.

Wilson, Marvin, R. *Our Father Abraham: Jewish Roots of the Christian Faith.* Grand Rapids, MI: William B. Eerdmans Publishing Company and Dayton, OH: Center For Judaic-Christian Studies, 1989.

Ungerleider, Samuel. "Judaism's First Century Diversity." PBS. April 1998. http://www.pbs.org/wgbh/pages/frontline/shows/religion/portrait/judaism.html

Vander Laan, Ray & That the World May Know Ministries. "The Desert–Our Jewish Roots." Lecture, Focus on the Family.

Yehoshua, Avram. "Kingdom Violence: Matthew 11:12." (weblog post). The Seed of Abraham. September 12, 2014. http://SeedofAbraham.net

Young, Brad, H. *Jesus: The Jewish Theologian.* Peabody, MA: Hendrickson Publishers, Inc., 1995.

Young, Brad, H. *Meet The Rabbis: Rabbinic Thought and the Teachings of Jesus.* Grand Rapids, MI: Baker Academic, 2007.

Young, Brad, H. *The Parables; Jewish Tradition and Christian Interpretation.* Grand Rapids, MI: Baker Academic, Baker Publishing Group, 1998.

Zavada, Jack. "Herod the Great – Ruthless King of the Jews." (weblog post). About.com Religion & Spirituality. http://christianity.about.com/od/newtestamentpeople/a/JZ-Herod-The-Great.htm

Ziegler, Paul. "The Blood Covenant." (weblog post). 2015. http://www.systemath.com/uploads/6/9/5/2/6952345/the-blood-covenant.pdf

Websites

To further your own study about Jesus in the Hebrew Scriptures and what it means for us today, check out these websites:

American-Israeli Cooperative Enterprise (AICE). (2015). Olive. *Jewish Virtual Library.* http://easybloom.com/plantlibrary/plant/olive

Jewish Encyclopedia. (2011). www.jewishencyclopedia.com

Rich, Tracey. (2012). *Judaism 101.* http://www.jewfaq.org/index.shtml

Tverberg, Lois (Host). *Our Rabbi Jesus: His Jewish Life and Teaching.* www.ourrabbijesus.com

Vander Laan, Ray (Host). That the World May Know Ministries: *Your Guide on a Journey through the World of Jesus.* https://www.thattheworldmayknow.com/

Worship Productions. (2014). www.ShepherdsInIsrael.com

Notes

Chapter 1: In The Beginning, Messiah

1. Michael Rydelnik, *The Messianic Hope* (B&H Academic, Nashville, Tennessee, 2010), 13–33.

2. Marvin R. Wilson, *Our Father Abraham* (Grand Rapids: Eerdmans Publishing company, 1989), 135–161.

Chapter 2: Abram's Unintended Covenant

1. James E. Smith, *The Pentateuch* (College Press, Joplin, Missouri, 2010), 130.

2. Ibid., 131.

3. Clay Trumbull, *The Blood Covenant* (Philadelphia, PA: John D. Wattles & Co., 1885).

4. Ibid.

5. James Garlow & Rob Price, *The Blood Covenant: The Story of God's Extraordinary Love for You* (Kansas City: Beacon Hill Press, 2013) 26.

6. Ibid., 188.

Chapter 3: Moses Gets the Water

1. "Judean Wilderness," Bible Places, www.bibleplaces.com/judeanwilderness.html.

2. Ray Vander Laan and That the World May Know Ministries, "The Desert" (from *Our Jewish Roots* from a Focus on the Family seminar).

3. Ibid., 278–279.

4. Alfred Edersheim, *The Temple, Its Ministry and Service* (Grand Rapids: Eerdmans Publishing Company, 1958) 275.

Chapter 4: Messiah's Seven Feasts

1. Carol Brooks, "The Feasts of Israel," http://www.inplainsite.org/html/seven_feasts_of_israel.html.

2. John J. Parsons, "The Jewish Holidays," http://www.hebrew4christians.com/Holidays/holidays.html.

3. "Passover," Jewish Encyclopedia, http://www.jewishencyclopedia.com/articles/11933-passover.

4. Let Us Reason Ministries, "What Does Leaven Represent in the Scripture," www.letusreason.org

5. William Cartan, *The Christians Manual* (London: Williams and Norgate, 1876), 227.

6. Heather McDougall, "The Pagan Roots of Easter," *The Guardian*, 2010, www.theguardian.com.

7. Samuele Bacchinocchi, *God's Festivals: Part II* (Barren Springs: 2001).

8. Rabbi S. M. Lehrman, *The Jewish Festivals* (London: Shapiro, Valentine & Co., 1956), 155.

9. Philip Goodman, *On This Day of Judgment* (Philadelphia: The Jewish Publication Society of America, 1970).

10. Naphtali Winter, *The High Holy Days* (Jerusalem: Leon Amiel Publishing, 1973), 54.

11. Irving Greenberg, *The Jewish Way: Living the Holidays* (New York: Summit Books 1988), 207–208.

12. Brooks, "The Feasts of Israel."

13. David Brickner, "Finding Jesus in the Feast of Tabernacles," CNN, <http://www.cbn.com/spirituallife/biblestudyandtheology/jewishroots/feast_of_tabernacles_jews_for_jesus_david_brickner.aspx.

Chapter 5: Jonah, Immersed in Ministry

1. Ray C. Stedman, "Jonah: The Reluctant Ambassador," Adventuring through the Bible, May 22, 1966, http://www.biblearchaeology.org/post/2008/09/04/Dagon-The-Philistine-Fish-God.aspx.

2. Erika Belibtreu, "Grisly Assyrian Record of Torture and Death," *Biblical Archaeology Society* (Jan/Feb 1991), http://www.cojs.org/pdf/grisly_assyrian.pdf.

3. Visual Bible Alive Resource Center, <http://www.visualbiblealive.com/stock_image.php?id=78540

4. J. Roskoski, "Dagon: The Philistine Fish God," September 4, 2008, <http://www.biblearchaeology.org/post/2008/09/04/Dagon-The-Philistine-Fish-God.aspx

5. H. Clay Trumbull, *Jonah in Nineveh*, (The Society of Biblical Literature: Journal of Biblical Literature, 1892, Vol. 11, No. 1), 56.

6. Steven M. Collins, Re: "Jonah-The Misunderstood Prophet" <http://www.stevenmcollins.com/articles/jonah-the-misunderstood-prophet/

7. Edward B. Davis, Re: "A Modern Jonah," December 1, 1991, <http://www.reasons.org/articles/a-modern-jonah

Chapter 6: The Branches

1. E.W.G. Masterman, "Olive Tree," <http://www.internationalstandardbible.com/O/olive-tree.html

2. EasyBloom.com, "Olive," < http://easybloom.com/plantlibrary/plant/olive

3. Walter C. Kaiser, *The Messiah in the Old Testament*, (Grand Rapids: Zondervan Publishing, 1995), 211-212.

4. Rydelnik, The *Messianic Hope*, 13-33.

5. Kaiser, The *Messiah In The Old Testament*, 213-217.

Chapter 7: Sheep, Shepherds, Goats

6. Shepherdsinisrael.com. "100-year old Photos Depict the Life of Shepherds in Ancient Palestine."

7. Follow the Rabbi, "The Lord Is My Shepherd," <http://v2.followtherabbi.com/journey/faith-lesson/the-lord-is-my-shepherd

8. Lynn Anderson, *They Smell Like Sheep*, (West Monroe: Howard Publishing, 1997), 12.

9. Ibid., p. 13.

Chapter 8: The Big Rock Religion of Caesarea Philippi

1. Raymond F. Culpepper & Floyd D. Carey, *No Church Left Behind*, (Cleveland: Pathway Press, 2007), 32.

2. Richard L. Matteoli, "Bestiality and Religion," *Salem-News*, June 26, 2013 <http://www.academia. edu/7152583/I-D_Bestiality_and_Religion

3. That The World May Know Ministries, (n.d.), "Fertility Cults of Canaan," <https:// www.thattheworldmayknow.com/ fertility-cults-of-canaan

Chapter 9: Saving a Wee Little Man

1. Natural Height Growth, "How Tall Is The Height of Jesus Christ?" <http://www. naturalheightgrowth.com/2012/12/20/ how-tall-is-the-height-of-jesus-christ/

2. Don Leichael, *Ipso Facto: A Scientific Exploration of the Old and New Testaments*, (Digital Publishing Centre, 2012). 434.

3. Samuel Kurinsky, "Jewish Traders of the Diaspora," *Hebrew History Federation* <http://www. hebrewhistory.info/factpapers/fp042-1_traders.htm

4. Bible History Online, (n.d.), "Ancient Tax Collectors," <http://www.bible-history.com/ sketches/ancient/tax-collector.html

Chapter 10: Saying No to the Greatest Ever

1. Jack Zavada, "Herod the Great–Ruthless King of the Jews," <http://christianity.about.com/od/newtestamentpeople/a/JZ-Herod-The-Great.htm

2. Ken Spiro, "Herod the Great," Judaism Online, Jewish History, <http://www.simpletoremember.com/articles/a/herod3_the_great/

3. Miriam C. Berkowitz, *Taking The Plunge: A Practical And Spiritual Guide To The Mikveh*, (Jerusalem: Schechter Institute of Biblical Studies, 2009).

4. David Flusser, *Judaism and the Origins of Christianity*, (Jerusalem: Magnes Press, 1988), 50-53, 140-141.

Chapter 11: A Tale of Two Gardens

1. The Jewish Virtual Library, "Garden of Eden," 2013, <https://www.jewishvirtuallibrary.org/jsource/judaica/ejud_0002_0007_0_07069.html

2. William Thomson, *The Land and The Book*, (London, 1859).

3. See The Holy Land, "Gethsemane," (2010), <http://www.seetheholyland.net/gethsemane/

4. Mark E. Jeffries, "The Coming of the Messiah," (Lulu.com, 2015).

Chapter 12: Seven Statements That Changed the World

1. Kaiser, *The Messiah In The Old Testament*, 178-181.

2. Job 21:20, Psalm 16:5, 23:5, 75:8, 116:13, Isaiah 51:17,22, Jeremiah 25:15, Ezekiel 23:32-33, Zechariah 12:2, Mark 10:38, 14:36

Chapter 15: The Seven Statements: Jesus Finishes His World

1. The Message of the Word of God, "Hyssop In Scripture," <http://www.amarel.com/hyssop_in_scripture.html

2. BibleStudy.org, "Why Did Jesus Refuse Wine Mixed With Gall," <http://www.biblestudy.org/question/why-did-jesus-refuse-to-drink-wine-with-gall-while-on-cross.html

Chapter 16: It's Saturday Night in the Upper Room

1. Smith's Bible Dictionary, "Hyssop," <http://www.biblestudytools.com/dictionaries/smiths-bible-dictionary/hyssop.html

2. David Flusser, *The Sage From Galilee*, (Grand Rapids: William B. Eerdmans Publishing Company, 2007), 140.

3. Lois Tverberg, *Walking In the Dust of Rabbi Jesus*, (Grand Rapids: Zondervan Publishing Company, 2012), 145-153.

4. Abraham Joshua Heschel, *God In Search of Man*, (New York: Farrar, Straus, Giroux, 1955), 3.